I Shall Arise

I SHALL ARISE

The life and ministry of
Donald A. Macfarlane

Edited by
JOHN TALLACH

Faro Publishing

FARO PUBLISHING
Aberdeen, Scotland.

© Faro Publishing 1984
First published 1984

ISBN 0 9509775 0 0

Distributed by:
EVANGELICAL PRESS
16—18 High Street, Welwyn, Hertfordshire,
AL6 9EQ, England.

Typeset in Great Britain by Inset, Chappel Hill, Chappel, Essex.
Printed by The Pitman Press, Bath, England.

Contents

Rejoice not against me, O mine enemy: when I fall,
I shall arise; *when I sit in darkness, the Lord*
shall be a light unto me . . .

He will bring me forth to the light, and I shall
behold his righteousness.

Then she that is mine enemy shall see it, and
shame shall cover her which said unto me,
Where is the Lord thy God?

Micah 7:8—10

Foreword

Rev D. A. Macfarlane was a minister of the Free Presbyterian Church of Scotland who was very warmly loved and highly respected within her borders. Gifted with a remarkable memory, deeply read in theology and related subjects, with a very wide general knowledge, he was an outstandingly humble man. Well qualified to minister the word and sacraments, he did this faithfully over a long ministry. His genuine humility led him to have a low estimate of his own work, and in consequence he wrote little for publication. In his later years, ill health prevented him from leaving home to labour outside his own congregation. As a result, knowledge of him and appreciation of his worth were comparatively confined.

John Tallach was a member of his congregation in his later years. In this book he has sought to share the privilege that gave him by refreshing the memory of those who knew Mr Macfarlane, and also by introducing his work to those who never knew him or heard him preach.

Mr Macfarlane's unique style of preaching, in which exposition cast original and striking lights on his subject — these lights often giving place to one another very quickly — demanded close attention and appreciation from the hearer. This, together with the fact that his preaching was delivered from a spirit steeped in devotion and was mingled with much material to give his hearers matter for their prayers, means that his sermons are difficult to transfer adequately to the printed page.

By judicious editing, John has performed well the difficult task of giving those who did not have the privilege of hearing

1

Mr Macfarlane preach a genuine impression of the man and his message. I do hope that those who were not thus privileged, as well as those who were, will find in this affectionate record of his life and some of his work a sweet savour of Christ which will encourage them to follow Mr Macfarlane's Master in the same spirit of meekness which Mr Macfarlane himself so obviously exhibited.

Rt. Hon. Lord Mackay of Clashfern
P.C., Q.C., LL.D.

Preface

When I was a boy in Mr Macfarlane's congregation in Dingwall, I came to know a Mr Docter, from Holland, who used to visit Scotland from time to time. He had come to appreciate Mr Macfarlane's ministry long before I first met him — in fact, long before I was born.

My mother used occasionally to send Mr Docter notes of sermons by Mr Macfarlane. I remember a letter of thanks which she once received from Mr Docter. As far as I can recall, he told in that letter how he had come in from a tiring day at work and had been delighted to find my mother's letter awaiting him, with the notes of Mr Macfarlane's address. He then described feelings like those of a hungry man eagerly sitting down to a meal but pausing first to say, 'Lord, bless this food'.

A book like this can only provide scraps from a ministry which extended over fifty-nine years. But I believe that even these scraps will prove spiritually nourishing to those who take them up in the spirit of Mr Docter's prayer:
Lord, bless this food.

John Tallach
Aberdeen
August 1984

3

Part One

Union Street, Aberdeen, at the beginning of the century. King Street, where Mr Macfarlane lodged, turns left off the end of Union Street. (Photograph from the G.W. Wilson collection, by kind permission of the Aberdeen University Library.)

1.
Biographical sketch

Background and early days

About the beginning of the nineteenth century, the Island
of Lewis lay under an almost pagan darkness. But, as the
century wore on, the Spirit of God began to send preachers
there to do a great work.

The first of these was Alexander Macleod, who went to
the parish of Uig on the west coast of Lewis in 1824. Under
Mr Macleod's ministry there came a spiritual awakening so
widespread that one visitor was able to testify, 'One *hears*
of religion elsewhere, but one *sees* it here in everything'.

In 1831 Robert Finlayson was settled as minister in the
parish of Lochs, on the east side of Lewis. Here he set to
work with all the zeal of a pioneer missionary, walking
endless miles over trackless moors and crossing the countless
inlets of the sea which fragmented his vast parish. Then, as
with his colleague on the other side of the island, God began
to work in a mighty way through his labours. In some respects the preaching of Robert Finlayson was unusual, and
even quaint. His use of allegory earned for him the title
'the John Bunyan of the Highlands'. But he excelled in
illustrating and enforcing the main doctrines of Scripture,
and he lived a life of exceptional nearness to his Lord.
A brother minister said 'Never did we feel the power of
personal holiness in re-enforcing the truth spoken from
the pulpit more than when hearing him'.

Meanwhile on another Hebridean island, Jura, a Donald
Macfarlane worked as a missionary. At this eventful time
in the spiritual history of Lewis, he was sent to help Mr
Finlayson in Lochs. While he worked as a missionary with

Mr Finlayson, he and his wife had a son. This is the background to one particular entry in the *Register of Baptisms* for the parish of Lochs:

> There was baptised by the Rev. Robert Finlayson to Donald Macfarlane, residing at Lacksay and Catherine Macfarlane, his lawful wife, a son: born 26th July, 1842, named Alexander.

The Macfarlanes soon went back to Jura; so Alexander did not stay long on the island on which he was born. But as he grew up in Jura, his father made sure that he heard of the many things God did in Lochs through the minister who baptised him there in 1842.

After a number of years Alexander left home to study at the Teacher Training College in Edinburgh. When he had completed his training, his first experiences as a teacher were gained in the island of Skye. After a time he was put in charge of the small school on Raasay. On this small, attractive island between Skye and the mainland he lived and worked for forty years.

As his father before him had known great ministers of the gospel, Alexander now enjoyed this privilege too. He often heard the famous Roderick Macleod of Snizort preach and his relationship with the outstanding Alexander MacColl, latterly of Lochalsh, was a very close one. He used to say that, when Mr MacColl preached, the time passed so quickly that one was always surprised when he stopped. His preaching was so attractive to believers that one girl of sixteen used to walk through the Saturday night from Applecross to Lochalsh to hear him. In 1882 Alexander Macfarlane married the daughter of a cousin of Mr MacColl's. He was forty years old at this time, and she was thirty-one.

Mr Macfarlane belonged to the Free Church of Scotland, which had been formed at the Disruption of 1843. As the last decade of the century approached, there were developments in the Free Church which caused concern to a number of its members and office bearers. One indication of these changes was the passing of a Declaratory Act in 1892. Some felt that the passing of this Act involved a weakening of the

Free Church's commitment to the Westminster Confession of Faith, with a consequent change for the worse in the constitution of the Church. This issue led in fact to the formation, in 1893, of the Free Presbyterian Church of Scotland. The minister who took the leading part in the formation of this new denomination was the Rev. Donald Macfarlane, who had just been inducted as the minister of Raasay in the spring of 1893. The new minister of Raasay and the elder in the schoolhouse had the same attitude to the Declaratory Act, and both were members of the first Presbytery of the Free Presbyterian Church of Scotland which met in July, 1893.

The vast majority of the people on the island of Raasay joined the Free Presbyterian Church along with their minister, but this did not prevent their minister's having to leave his manse. Since the granting of a suitable site for another manse on Raasay was delayed, Rev. D. Macfarlane lived for five years in Broadford on Skye. At the weekends he crossed the stretch of water between the two islands and stayed in the schoolhouse on Raasay. About this time Mrs Alexander Macfarlane, wife of the schoolmaster, had a severe attack of flu which seemed to weaken her to such an extent that she never fully recovered her strength. However, throughout these five years, she willingly gave hospitality to her minister; and he afterwards wrote that 'the kindness of Mrs Macfarlane and her husband to me during this time at Raasay is more than I can express in words.'

The first two children born to the Macfarlanes in the Raasay schoolhouse were girls. Then, on the 30th of March, 1889 — the year when Mr Macfarlane's friend Alexander MacColl died — a boy was born. They called him Donald Alexander.

When his older sister, Nellie, left home to attend high school, Donald became particularly close to his other sister, Catherine. Together they got up to some dangerous escapades, as they explored the shoreline beneath the schoolhouse.

One incident, from these early years in the Raasay schoolhouse, stood out afterwards in Donald's memory. The minister, the Rev. Donald Macfarlane, was visiting the schoolhouse. The schoolmaster had gone out of the room, and the visitor

thought that he had been left alone. He was warming his
hands at the fire, but in an agitated way, saying as he did
so, 'The carnal mind, the carnal mind is enmity against
God'. Actually there was a little boy watching and listening. When the boy told this incident as an old man he said,
'I had no idea then what the carnal mind was — unless it
was a bad tempered horse that used to live at the back of
the schoolhouse — but, whatever it was, I thought that,
if I could only get hold of it, there was nothing I would
not do to it for troubling Mr Macfarlane!'

Raasay School was not of sufficient size to offer higher
education, and in any case higher education was not provided by the state then as it is now. However, Donald won
two scholarships to Kingussie High School in Inverness-
shire. The headmaster of this school at the time was a Dr
Mackenzie, a gifted and dedicated teacher who was renowned
for the personal interest which he took in all his pupils.
Donald attended Kingussie High School for several years,
studying Latin and Greek as well as the other usual subjects.

From Kingussie Donald went to university, first at
Glasgow and then at Aberdeen. (The change to Aberdeen
was probably arranged because, during the course of Donald's
studies, his parents came from the west coast to live in Inverness. Aberdeen was nearer to Inverness than Glasgow was,
and it may also have been significant that the cost of lodgings
was lower in Aberdeen than in Glasgow.)

Conversion and call to the ministry

While studying in Glasgow during 1907—8 Donald frequently
called at the house of an Angus Macphail who came from
Jura and who knew his father well. During one of these
visits the conversation turned to the Gaelic language, and
Mr Macphail said to Donald that if he was to become a
minister he would need to learn Gaelic. Donald replied, 'If
I were to become a minister, I would need something more
than Gaelic.'

In the summer of 1909, while on holiday from university,
Donald was employed for a short time as a teacher in Torran,
at the north end of Raasay. It seems that it was during this

period that Donald came to possess that 'something more than Gaelic'. Now he began to relate in a living and personal way to the gospel which he had been taught from his early childhood. Apart from what he heard through his father and others, he was helped by reading *The Anxious Enquirer* by John Angel James.*

As Donald now became clearer about his own salvation, he became more concerned for that of his sister Nellie, who had by now married a banker and settled in Kyle. The following are extracts from a letter he wrote to Nellie after his return to Aberdeen for the summer term in April 1910:

> c/o Fraser,
> 607 King Street,
> Aberdeen

Darling Brother and Sister,
    I feel a bit lonely these days, I must confess — newly from home. I enjoyed my stay at home this time very much . . . (I had to stop there to light the gas.)
    I see that Mark Twain is dead. Not many years ago, he thought of dying at seventy. But when seventy came he took a second thought, he said, and intended to live on to a hundred. He had wonderful literary powers, but it is doubtful if he had the power of life and death.
    I had a letter from home this week and they are as well as can be expected. Mama is slowly getting better, I hope. It was on a very cold Sabbath night, I think, that she caught a chill.
    I am, it may be by spurts and starts, learning that there is one thing which is needful — absolutely needful — although we don't desire this one thing needful. We never worship God as *natural* rational beings. This is a hard, harsh statement; but I am unable to delete a word of it . . .

In the latter part of the letter Donald speaks about the need to believe in Christ and says, 'You don't, Nellie, take

*This book was reprinted in 1976 by Baker Book House under the title *Being Born Again.*

a year to believe that the sun is shining.' He must have been afraid that the letter would not be too well received by his older sister, as he closes with the appeal: 'Don't skim over the latter part of this letter, Nellie.'

When Donald writes about enjoying his recent stay at home he is of course referring to Inverness, not Raasay. His father had retired the previous summer and both his parents had come to live in Fairfield Road, Inverness. He speaks also about his mother being unwell, and expresses the hope that she will soon be better. Sadly, she died just two days after that letter was written. Her last words were the two lines from Psalm 115:

> *The Lord of us hath mindful been*
> *And He will bless us still.*

At the end of that summer term Donald graduated at Aberdeen with an M.A. Degree. By this time he felt that he was being called to the ministry, and he was received as a divinity student of his Church.

Afterwards, when discussing what constitutes a call to the ministry, Mr Macfarlane spoke of how some people may present a text as the basis for their claim to have a call to the ministry — 'and perhaps the text has been dragged backwards out of context'. Mr Macfarlane did not share the view that having such a particular 'text' was the matter of supreme importance in judging whether or not a man did have a call to the ministry. He attached more importance to the desire for the gospel ministry which the Spirit gives to all whom he calls, and quoted with approval the phrase from a writer whose views on this matter he shared: 'a desire such that it would be painful to extinguish'. Probably we can deduce something about Mr Macfarlane's own call from these general views of his on the subject.

Because his denomination was a small one, and the number of divinity students few, the system for training in divinity was that students should study for a period with each of two tutors who were ministers with congregations of their own. The tutors in charge of the training of students at that time were Rev. J. R. Mackay, Inverness, and Rev. D. Beaton, Wick. Both of them were learned men and gifted tutors.

The Rev. (later Professor) J. R. Mackay was an outstanding scholar who taught his students theology from the Latin text of Turretin's *Works*. Perhaps some students were not able to derive the greatest possible benefit from this approach, but Mr Macfarlane would have enjoyed it greatly. Mr Mackay once remarked, 'Mr Macfarlane has such a capacious mind that you can pour all you have into it and it will hold it all — and more!'

The summer of 1911 was spent in Fort William, where Mr Macfarlane held the services for the small F.P. congregation. Another summer was similarly spent in North Uist. So the four years of his theological training passed, and he was ready to be ordained as a minister in the summer of the year when the Great War began.

Darkness and light

On the 14th of August, 1914, Mr Macfarlane was ordained and inducted to his first pastoral charge. His congregation was made up of four parts, each with its own church building — Lairg and Bonar, Dornoch and Rogart. Cars were a rare possession in those days. Most of Mr Macfarlane's travelling was therefore done on foot, though he sometimes had the use of a horse and trap. He would spend a weekend in turn at each of the four stations, staying on for a day or two to visit the people in that area.

At first he lodged in Rogart, but when a manse was built at Lairg he stayed there. He was still unmarried, so his father and his sister Catherine left Inverness and took up residence with him in the new Lairg manse. This arrangement was helpful in more ways than one. There was a great need for preaching supply because of the large number of services held throughout the congregation every week. His father had heard and known great preachers during his Christian life, and could put this privilege to use while preaching himself. An experienced teacher with an orderly mind, he had the gift of presenting his subject in a way that his hearers could understand. As the years passed the congregation grew attached, not to their minister only, but to his father as well.

Mr Macfarlane remained the pastor of that scattered congregation for seven years, and then he accepted a call which came to him from the congregation of Oban. His sister and father (now almost eighty years of age), both accompanied Mr Macfarlane when he went to that picturesque town on the west coast of Scotland in June, 1921.

Alexander MacColl, the Highland preacher already referred to, once asked in the course of a sermon 'What kind of minister would you like as your minister?' The answer he gave to his own question was: 'For myself I would like that minister who had been scorched by the law, melted by the gospel, and much sifted by the temptations of Satan.' Oban was the place where Mr Macfarlane began to experience in a very painful way the siftings of Satan. Reflecting on what he had passed through around the summer of 1909 when he had been teaching at Torran, he began to feel that his experience then must have been very superficial. Satan made use of that strong tendency to introspection which was natural to him. Before long Mr Macfarlane was doubting whether he knew the Lord or not. He began to feel that he had been given only temporary faith, that he was still a stranger to saving faith. Naturally these crippling temptations had the severest repercussions on his ministry, and when it came to the autumn of 1927 he was unable to preach. He had a nervous breakdown.

By now Mr Macfarlane had a secure place in the hearts and prayers of those who had come to appreciate his ministry; and in this time of trial they did not let him down. His elderly colleague, minister of St. Jude's congregation in Glasgow, wrote to him on 19th September:

216 West Regent Street,
Glasgow

My dear Mr Macfarlane,
    You are very often in my thoughts and words at the throne of grace. It is written: 'Who shall lay any thing to the charge of God's elect? It is God that justifieth. Who is he that condemneth? It is Christ that died, yea rather that is risen again, who is even at the right hand

of God, who also maketh intercession for us.' Christ
came on very purpose into this world to seek and to
save *that which was lost.* Do you not believe that he
is able to save any sinner — then, *why not you?* Cheer
up, my dear friend, for there is forgiveness with God.
'This is a faithful saying, and worthy of all acceptation,
that Christ Jesus came into the world to save sinners;
of whom I am chief.' May the Lord lift the light of his
countenance on your soul. With kindest regards and
sympathy,

> Yours in the bonds of the gospel,
> Neil Cameron

On 13th October Mr Cameron wrote again saying,

You are very often in my thoughts since we parted at
Connel Station. I do hope that the Lord has of his great
mercy sent his word to heal your wounded heart. I can
enter fully into your painful experience — of darkness,
doubts, fears, and other trying temptations — and
therefore can truly sympathize with you. The Lord can
and will in his own good time deliver your soul out of
this darkness, even by one passage of scripture. I always
found it so and I am convinced you will do so too . . .

That reference to Connel station probably indicates that,
by this time, Mr Macfarlane was living at Connel village, a
few miles out of Oban. Apparently the doctor had ordered
a change of scenery, and he had accordingly come to stay
there, at the house of a Captain Noble. However a change
of scenery was not enough; so Mr Macfarlane again moved,
this time to Glasgow, and stayed at a private nursing home
in South Park Terrace. No doubt part of the purpose behind
this move to Glasgow was to be near Rev. Neil Cameron.
Meanwhile Andrew Cameron, one of his elders back in
Oban, wrote to Mr Macfarlane, 'hoping to hear good news
soon'. And it was not only the people of his own congregation who were following him through this trying period
with their prayers. A Mrs Fraser wrote from 18 Crown
Street, Inverness:

My dear Mr Macfarlane,

I do not consider myself worthy of writing, but at the same time I would think it unkind of me if I did not do it. We were all very sorry to hear of your being so low in mind. We believe it will all be for your eternal good. The Lord's people will have reason to praise him for his chastisements as well as for his comforts. When you took ill first I had portions of scripture that would come before my mind, like Malachi 3:3, 'And he shall sit as a refiner and purifier of silver, and he shall purify the sons of Levi, and purge them as gold and silver, that they may offer unto the Lord an offering in righteousness.'

Dear Mr Macfarlane, we hope that the winter may soon be past and that you may hear the voice of the turtle and that the time of the singing of birds will come. Oh what need we all have that we would hear his blessed voice . . . We are sure that the Lord is your shield and your exceeding great reward — although you are at present walking in darkness.

My aunt and my husband join in sending love to you.

But Mr Macfarlane's depression continued, and in that state he went back to the Oban area. Again he stayed a few miles from Oban, at Connel, this time at the house of a Mr and Mrs MacSween who opened their home in a spirit of Christian love in the time of their minister's need. Sometimes, when going upstairs to bed, Mr Macfarlane would give his personal effects to Mr MacSween to look after as he felt sure that he was going to die before the morning.

The doctor did not know how to help Mr Macfarlane and about this time he suggested that a private nurse be employed to look after him. So Nurse MacAra came to Connel, and a greater contrast between nurse and patient could hardly be imagined. She was Irish, she dressed in the latest fashion, and she smoked! Many an hour she spent, during that spring of 1928, sitting across the fire from her patient. She had a strong personality, and she adopted shock tactics in an attempt to take him out of himself.

At last the doctor decided that what Mr Macfarlane

required was a combination of the care of this forceful nurse and a complete separation from his normal environment. So Mr Macfarlane and Miss MacAra packed their respective cases and set off for Crieff. He had no friends there. But it was in that lonely spot that God met Mr Macfarlane in a special way, giving him spiritual comfort and taking the burden off his mind. The words which were the means of bringing him this blessing were 'I shall not die, but live and declare the works of the Lord. The Lord hath chastened me sore; but he hath not given me over unto death.' (Psalm 118: 17,18)

Psalm 130 also became precious to Mr Macfarlane, and one can see how utterly suited to his case the words of this psalm were: 'Out of the depths have I cried unto thee O Lord . . . If thou, Lord, shouldest mark iniquities, O Lord, who shall stand? But there is forgiveness with thee, that thou mayest be feared . . . My soul waiteth for the Lord, more than they that watch for the morning . . . Let Israel hope in the Lord: for with the Lord there is mercy, and with him is plenteous redemption. And he shall redeem Israel from all his iniquities.'

It seems that, characteristically, Mr Macfarlane went to see what Owen had to say on this passage of scripture. And he was so delighted with what he found that he tore out the page which was of particular help to him, and carried it around for years in his jacket pocket. The pages number 603/604 in Volume 6 of Owen's *Works*, where Owen is concluding his comments on verse 4 of Psalm 130, and is dealing with *Objections to believing from the power of sin.* In this passage Owen deals with the temptation which believers may have that they have never really known forgiveness of sin because, if they had, sin would not now be working so powerfully in their hearts. He gives various reasons why these actings of indwelling sin are so perplexing to the believer. It seems that the following remarks by Owen were of particular comfort to Mr Macfarlane.

(The actings of indwelling sin are perplexing) because they are *unexpected*. The soul looks not for them upon the first great conquest made of sin, and universal engagement of the heart unto God. When it first says

'I have sworn, and am steadfastly purposed to keep thy righteous judgments' commonly there is peace, at least for a season, from the disturbing vigorous actings of sin. There are many reasons why so it should be. 'Old things are then passed away, all things are become new.' And the soul, under the power of that universal change, is utterly turned away from those things that should foment, stir up, provoke, or cherish any lust or temptation. Now, when some of these advantages are past, and sin begins to stir and act again, the soul is surprised, and thinks the work that he has passed through was not true and effectual, but temporary only; yea, he thinks, perhaps, that sin hath more strength than it had before, because he is more sensible than he was before. As one that hath a dead arm or limb, whilst it is mortified, endures deep cuts and lancings, and feels them not; so when spirits and sense are brought into the place again, he feels the least cut, and may think the instruments sharper than they were before, when all the difference is, that he hath got a quickness of sense, which before he had not. It may be so with a person in this case: he may think lust more powerful than it was before, because he is more sensible than he was before. Yea, sin in the heart is like a snake or serpent: you may pull out the sting of it, and cut it into many pieces; though it can sting mortally no more, nor move its whole body at once, yet it will move in all its parts, and make an appearance of a greater motion than formerly. So it is with lust: when it hath received its death wound, and is cut to pieces, it moves in so many parts as it were in the soul, that it amazes him that hath to do with it; and thus coming unexpectedly, fills the spirit oftentimes with disconsolation.

Similarly underlined and commented on are the following passages from page 603:

. . . and even whilst his people are sinning, he can find something in their hearts, words, or ways, that pleaseth him; much more in their duties. He is a skilful refiner, that can find much gold in that ore where we see nothing but lead or clay. He remembers the duties which we forget, and forgets the sins which we remember. He justifies our persons, though ungodly; and will also our duties, though not perfectly godly.

To give a little further support in reference unto our wretched, miserable duties, unto them that are in perplexities on that account, know that *Jesus Christ takes whatever is evil and unsavoury out of them, and makes them acceptable.* When an unskilful servant gathers many herbs, flowers and weeds in a garden, you gather them out that are useful, and cast the rest out of sight. Christ deals so with our performances. All the ingredients of self that are in them on any account he takes away, and adds incense to what remains, and presents it to God, Exodus 30:36. This is the cause that the saints at the last day, when they meet their own duties and performances, know them not, they are so changed from what they were when they went out of their hand. 'Lord, when saw we thee naked or hungry?' So that God accepts a little, and Christ makes our little a great deal.

The news of his deliverance caused great rejoicing among those who had upheld Mr Macfarlane in prayer throughout his trial. From Rogart, in his former congregation, a Johan MacMaster wrote on the 18th of April, 1928: 'Glory be to God for the good news that I expected and longed for.' Another letter was sent in the same month from the far north of Scotland:

> The Cottage,
> Halkirk,
> Caithness

Dear Sir,
    Friends here were relieved to know that you were loosed from your bonds and restored to your home and congregation. There were more praying for you than you knew. In speaking of you to Mr James Campbell, builder, Inverness, I remarked that you

could not accept comfort unless it came from the Lord
to yourself. He said, 'Isn't that good?' and spoke very
feelingly about you.

. . . I notice about the 12th of Isaiah that there is a
call to prayer, preaching, singing and shouting — that
is, to all the exercises of worship — after deliverance.

I would like to read Owen on the 130th Psalm.
I haven't the book, but will get it from Mr Beaton when
I go to the Wick communion, if well.

With best wishes and kind remembrances from Halkirk
friends,

Yours very sincerely,
Georgina Sinclair

Another letter came from Edinburgh:

7 Lower Granton Road,
Leith

April 3rd, 1928

My dear Mr Macfarlane,

Words of mine cannot convey to you the joy your
letter gave to me — I had to lay it down three times
before I could finish reading it. Then I felt like Billy
Bray: I could shout 'Glory, Glory, Glory!' . . .

Our hearts are deceitful above all things. But when
we get a clear call for duty from his own word we
must hasten to obey. I heard a sermon once on 'The
heart is deceitful above all things . . .' and it revealed
to me such depravity in my own heart that I seemed to
be rooted to my seat. I managed to stand at the last
prayer and before it was over I got such a faith's view
of the Lamb of God in his absolute sufficiency to
cleanse and pardon that it was a happy day for me.
I do not often open my mind in this way, but you
will know why I tell you this and speak as I do. It is
not of the will of the flesh that love is put into our
souls towards one another; it is from God. Satan will
get in at every door if he can; but where the foundation
is, he cannot get.

I heard you in Stratherrick on the vineyard of the

slothful, and what a heap of weeds turned up in mine! Unbelief is the giant that is so strong, for it seems to push out everything before it when reigning. Your remark on our inability to wash at the fountain until power comes from the Father to appropriate the spiritual efficacy of the divine atonement was very precious to me. When that comes, unbelief will have to go.

I was thinking of you during the night and got such a lot from finding myself sorrowing for one who was sorrowing that the experience became a very hallowed one for me.

I got word today to go into hospital again, so likely they will operate D.V. very soon. If I have the sweet assurance of God's love, all will be well. May I get grace to rest on the Lord Jesus . . .

My deep thanks for your letter, and that you may be given back to us as a Church is my loving and sincere desire.

D. W. Mackenzie

Andrew Cameron (the elder from whose letter a brief quotation was given above) had an attractive and capable daughter, Catherine. Two of Catherine's sisters did not enjoy good health. This meant that Catherine's ageing parents depended very much on her support. So that when Mr Macfarlane came along and explained that he would like to marry Catherine, Mr and Mrs Cameron found it difficult to take this proposal in their stride. Actually this friendship had begun between the minister and the elder's daughter some time before, but only now that Mr Macfarlane's breakdown had passed could marriage be spoken of. They were married in August, 1928. The bridesmaid was one of the ladies who ran the nursing home in Glasgow where Mr Macfarlane had been shown great kindness during the previous winter.

Catherine Cameron was a cheerful, practical Christian whose personality and outlook made her an invaluable help to Mr Macfarlane. It was a particularly kind providence which opened the way to Mr Macfarlane's marriage at this time, both in relation to the trouble through which he had recently passed and also in view of the loss which he was soon to sustain. His father was by now quite elderly and frail, and on the last Sabbath of January, 1930, he passed away. So the end came for one who had been baptised by Robert Finlayson, and his death meant the breaking of a link with great preachers and great gospel days in the history of the Highlands. He had been a devoted father, supporting his son with mature advice and earnest, loving prayer.

Shortly after this, Mr Macfarlane was approached by the joint congregation of Dingwall and Beauly, in Ross-shire. He felt led to accept this request to become their pastor, and was inducted by the Northern Presbytery on the 15th of May, 1930.

One of the members of his new congregation who was particularly glad that he came to Dingwall was only nine years of age at the time. Soon after Mr Macfarlane arrived this girl, Helen, became ill with rheumatic fever. More than anything else, it was Mr Macfarlane's visits which brightened what was otherwise a long and dreary period. After that illness, as well as many others through which she passed as a child, she used to think 'It is almost worth being ill to have Mr Macfarlane's visits!'

It was not that Mr Macfarlane could relate to children by telling them funny stories or playing with them. It was just that his desire for Helen's good communicated itself to her in a direct and powerful way. She remembers how once, after he had spoken and prayed with her and left the room, he put his head back round the door and quoted the words, 'Thou wilt keep him in perfect peace whose mind is stayed on thee, because he trusteth in thee.' When he said things like that, there was an indescribable authority about it. One felt that nothing more could be said, or needed to be said.

During the period of his ministry in Ross-shire Mr Macfarlane became known throughout the area as a practical Christian. There are many examples of how he showed his concern for others. On one occasion, he came across two cars parked beside the road. He stopped his own car and asked if he could help. One of the men explained that his car had run out of petrol and that they wished to transfer petrol from one car to the other, but they had no tin into which the petrol could be siphoned. Mr Macfarlane promptly took off his hat and told them to make use of it!

During the war, he and his wife were visiting in the Black Isle where they were given a present of two rabbits. The manse had a constant stream of visitors, and in those days of meat rationing Mrs Macfarlane was especially thankful to have this extra food. However, Mr Macfarlane was thinking of others who were in need too, and before they had got back to Dingwall he had given both rabbits away!

Teaching Greek and Hebrew

Another aspect of Mr Macfarlane which could not but strike those who got to know him was his outstanding intellectual gifts. Where others struggled to remember, he did not seem able to forget. He seemed to know a lot about nearly everything; and as far as subjects relating to the work of the ministry were concerned, his knowledge was quite astounding.

He studied theology constantly. All his volumes by the Puritans, like Owen and Charnock, were read and re-read. The fly leaves and the margins were crowded with jottings of thoughts which suggested themselves to him while reading, or with cross-references to other passages in the book. It seemed that whenever anyone raised a question with Mr Macfarlane he was able to go over to his shelves, pick out the volume he wanted, and turn to the spot where the point in question was dealt with, perhaps by Calvin, Owen, Charles Hodge, or Warfield.

Despite this vast store of knowledge, his natural tendency was to conceal how much he knew. But on occasions it could not be hidden. He was once stopped on the street in Dingwall by a minister who asked for his help in understanding a particular passage in Acts. Mr Macfarlane was able to give the help requested there and then — by explaining the significance of precisely how this passage was punctuated in Greek. On another occasion a divinity student called on Mr Macfarlane. As they discussed the passages which this student was at the time studying in his Hebrew class, he was not a little surprised to find that, to Mr Macfarlane, it seemed almost as easy to quote a passage in Hebrew as in English!

It is not surprising that when, in 1932, the Synod of the Free Presbyterian Church was seeking someone to tutor its divinity students in Greek and Hebrew, Mr Macfarlane was appointed for this work. This meant that, when students were at that stage of their training when they studied these languages and related subjects, they would join his class in Dingwall. His estimate of the standards required in anyone carrying out this important work was such that he made it a condition of his acceptance that he would first be allowed to go to London for extra study. Here he received advanced training in Hebrew for six months, and his tutor started this particularly apt pupil on the study of another Semitic language as well!

One of his students, the late Rev. Donald Campbell, M.A., Edinburgh, wrote in appreciation of Mr Macfarlane:

'A most pious man, Mr Macfarlane was greatly beloved and highly esteemed. The Lord's people thought of him as a prince in Israel and, like Nathanael, an Israelite indeed in whom there was no guile. Endowed with a brilliant intellect, he towered above many. He was, however, so clothed with humility that he regarded himself as the least of all saints.

'As one who had read so widely, including ecclesiastical history, and one so greatly blessed with a retentive memory, he was no small asset in church courts. Invaluable, however, as his contribution towards church government was, it was in the evangelical field that he excelled. As a preacher of the gospel he would figure with distinction among the "able ministers of the New Testament". While taking as his main theme Christ and him crucified Mr Macfarlane, like his Master, led his flock gently, carrying the lambs in his bosom. Never wittingly did he press the Lord's people beyond their strength, and when they were cast down through manifold temptations few were more helpful than he in tenderly binding up their wounds. One passing through a trial of soul affliction found him handling the case as though he had been told the details. His concluding words, "Cast yourself on the bed of his mercy," brought the oil of joy for mourning. Mr

Macfarlane was indeed a polished shaft in his Master's hand. Many will thank God to all eternity for his ability to penetrate the very depths of the soul, exposing what was offensive, and commending what the Lord had planted there. Like the apostle Peter he was commissioned to feed Christ's sheep and lambs, and he never wearied in directing sinners to Jesus the Saviour.

'By any standards, Mr Macfarlane was highly qualified for the work of a theological tutor. Two prominent features of his fitness were his own masterly grasp of Hebrew and Greek, and his ability to assess a student's intellectual capacity. Accordingly, he set the pace of the class expecting everybody to give of his best. The one with five talents should work according to his gifts, and so should the one with two, while no one was permitted to bury his talent in the earth. His ability to impart knowledge was impressive. This proved a great advantage to his students, whose achievements he made his responsibility. When the exam results were good, the tutor enthusiastically shared with his students the pleasure of success. This engendered a mutual interest in the work, and proved an incentive to even greater effort until the course was completed. His insistence on his students' reaching an acceptable standard came from his conviction that the preparation for the office of the ministry should be of the best. While stressing the importance of the educational aspect, of course, he always gave the pre-eminence to grace.

'True to his Christian profession and noble character, Mr Macfarlane treated his fellow men with becoming courtesy. This indeed was an outstanding feature of his whole life. Without compromising his own principles, he was all things to all men. '

'In any other profession, one with his intellectual capacity could have attained to high distinction. Ambition for fame, however, was alien to Mr Macfarlane. Like Moses, he chose rather to suffer affliction with the people of God than to pursue the doubtful pleasures which worldly fame brings. He found

satisfaction in serving the Lord as a minister of the
gospel, and regarded this as a divinely bestowed honour.
In the ministerial office he had scope and opportunity
both to use his talents and apply his knowledge to a
better understanding of the great themes which the
gospel of Christ supplies.'

Further trials

Once more, however, a shadow came over his life. In 1955,
his wife died. He had become so dependent on her that he
felt quite lost. Added to this severe blow, he took flu twice
within a short space of time. When Mr Macfarlane was thus
physically and nervously weakened, Satan came to get an
advantage over him. Again he entered a dark period of
doubt, and suffered a second nervous breakdown. For
months he was unable to preach.

He was taken to hospital in Inverness, and the treatment
he received there proved of real help to him. (About ten
years after this, a young Christian medical student was
working for a short period at this mental hospital. Over
coffee one day, he came round to discussing religion with
a charge nurse who was an unbeliever and ridiculed the
Christian faith. 'And yet,' he told the young student, 'there
was one man who made me think − a minister who came
into my ward from Dingwall years ago. I'll admit to you
that I felt *he* had something genuine.')

Mr Macfarlane was fond of the writings of Thomas Haly-
burton (which he regarded as a kind of 'Owen simplified').
When he felt somewhat better, he was reading Halyburton's
Works and was glad to come across a paragraph* where
Halyburton deals with *Man's recovery by faith in Christ:*

. . . We do here, in the name of our great Lord and
Master, offer him for wisdom, righteousness, sanctification, and redemption: we offer him, and all he
has, to every one within these doors. Whoever he be,
whatever your sins are, though as great as ever were

*On page 188 of the single volume edition published in 1833.

the sins of any of the sons of Adam, we do here offer Christ to you, and do promise, that if you will accept of him, he will 'in no wise cast you out'; nay, he shall save you, make you sons of God, nay, heirs, yea, and joint heirs with himself. 'Believe in the Lord Jesus and ye shall be saved.' Take him, and have him; take him, and have him with all things; all the blessings that the infinite, eternal, electing love of the Father designed for his chosen ones; all the blessings that the precious blood of God, one drop whereof was of more value than ten thousand worlds, did purchase; all that the great and precious promises of the life that now is, and of that which is to come, are able to grasp or comprehend; all that quick-sighted faith that looks from one eternity to another, from eternal electing love projecting mercy, to eternal salvation, flowing from that fountain, can set its eye upon; all that the enlarged capacity of a perfected soul can hold or desire to all eternity; in one word, all that a God can bestow, or a creature receive; if ye receive Christ, all is and shall be yours.

Also, reading on page 189/90, he was helped by words Halyburton addressed to 'You who, after search, are in doubt about yourselves whether you do believe or not.' There he read:

Conclude not that ye want faith, because ye do not see or find all these things in yourselves which others have found, either before, in the time, or after the Lord's working faith in them, whereby they are united to Christ. Some have a strong law-work, of long continuance, before conversion; some have much distinctness, confidence, and clearness, at the very time of conversion, which enables them to give a distinct account of the time, place, and means of their conversion; and some have much joy and high manifestations afterwards. But though ye come not their length, ye have no reason thence to conclude yourselves unbelievers, since in some the exercise is neither so intense, nor of such continuance, as that of others, only it is such as is sufficient to take them out of themselves to Christ; and this is all the sense of sin that is absolutely necessary. Some cannot, amidst the mist raised by their own corruptions, Satan, and the world, see God working upon their souls; nor can they reach that joy and comfort in believing, which others do. . .

Study the nature of the covenant of grace well. This will be exceedingly helpful to you, and remove many rubs out of your way, and answer many of your doubts; particularly, study to know the ground of your acceptance with God, and of your admission and access into a covenant-relation: it is not your freedom from sin, it is not freedom from gross sins, nor is it anything wrought in us, or by us, but only the sovereignly free grace of God in Christ, which glories in removing the greatest offences, and bestowing the choicest mercies upon the chief of sinners . . .

Study acquaintance with the springs of that covenant-peace which believers enjoy in their walk with God. It is not their own merit, but God's mercy; it is not their own blamelessness, but the efficacy of Christ's blood to take away spots; it is not the evenness of our walk, and our freedom from trips; but it is the testimony of a good conscience, bearing witness that it is our exercise to have and keep 'a conscience void of offence toward God and man,' by continual dependence on God in Christ, for mercy to remove sin, and grace to help in time of need. Endeavour to understand these things well, and you will then be soon eased of many of your fears . . .

Pray for the influence of that Spirit which searcheth the deep things of God, and can let in such a beam of light into the soul as will clear to you fully what is your state . . . .

These comments and exhortations by Halyburton became very precious to him; to the extent that, as with the page from the book by Owen, he now carried these pages from Halyburton's *Works* about with him for a long time after this depression passed. Also, the text which Halyburton quoted at the beginning of the above extract took a place beside Psalm 130 as a scripture which had become particularly meaningful to him: 'But of him are ye in Christ Jesus, who of God is made unto us wisdom, and righteousness, and sanctification, and redemption: that, according as it is written, He that glorieth, let him glory in the Lord.' (1 Cor. 1:30—31)

And again, as provision had been made for him before, provision was made for him now. In 1957 he married Ella Finlayson, a member in the Dingwall congregation and a domestic science teacher in Dingwall Academy. Humanly speaking, she became the means of extending a ministry which had become unspeakably precious to the people of Dingwall and Beauly. Her training and practical experience were of great use to her as she now took over the running of the Dingwall manse. But it was perhaps her informed interest in theological issues which made her a particularly suitable companion to Mr Macfarlane.

The year 1964 brought with it the jubilee of his ordination to the ministry. His congregation did not wish this occasion to pass unmarked, and word got through to Mr Macfarlane that a presentation was to be made. However, the effect of this news was the opposite of that intended. The past was brought back, and Mr Macfarlane's sense of shortcoming became very strong. He was even at the point of doubting his call to the ministry, when the Lord sent deliverance to him in a remarkable way. On the very morning of the day on which the presentation was due to be made, the September issue of *The Gospel Magazine* arrived. The Rev. H. M. Carson's Editorial proved of great help to Mr Macfarlane:

> There are Christians who are dogged by a feeling of guilt. It is often linked with one particular sin in the past which to them marked a disastrous spiritual lapse. It may have been years ago that the failure occurred. It may be that they have long since confessed and received forgiveness. And yet there are still times when the past looms afresh in their mind and suddenly the assurance of pardon becomes faint. Perhaps it comes

at a time of discouragement when spirits are low, and
there is a tendency to succumb to depression. It may
come at a time of spiritual failure so that the present
weakness is magnified by the recollection of the past.
Possibly it is in the midst of some enterprise for God
that the past sin comes to mind, and the present service
seems all at once to be an act of hypocrisy.

Clearly this state of affairs produces a most unhappy
experience; and indeed at times it not only robs the
Christian of the joy which is his birthright but almost
paralyses him spiritually. Prayer becomes a constant
round of morbid self-examination. Fellowship with
other Christians is spoiled for he can only compare
his own known sinfulness with what he imagines to
be the superior holiness of his friends. Clearly he is
in a condition which needs a healing word from God.

Now the first step he must take is to recognise the
hand of the devil. It is of course easy to see the devil
at work when he prompts the flesh, or when he presents to us the attractions of the world. It is not so
easy to detect his strategy when he is using doubt as
one of his powerful weapons. It is true that every lapse
into sin is a victory for Satan; but how much greater
his triumph if he uses our failure to make us doubt the
promises of God which speak of forgiveness. How
overwhelming is his victory if he succeeds in making
us doubt our very standing in God's sight, even though
in the past we had a rich assurance of our justification.

How then are we to meet these accusations of the
devil as he calls past sin to remembrance? He is well
named 'the accuser of the brethren' but there is no
need to submit to his accusations. We have not one
answer, but many. We have the promises of God's
word which are the inheritance of God's people.
Because we are the people of the covenant, the God
of the covenant who speaks these promises backs them
with His own character.

Now what do these promises say to just such a situation as this? Surely they speak of the width of God's
forgiveness. God does not select the sins He will forgive — 'He is faithful and just to forgive us our sins and to

cleanse us from all unrighteousness' (I John 1:9). These promises speak not only of pardon and restoration to favour but of cleansing. He both forgives and He also cleanses us completely. Nor is this cleansing a temporary erasing of a stain, for each time the devil tries to recall the sin of the past we hear God saying 'I have blotted out as a thick cloud thy transgressions and as a cloud thy sins' (Isaiah 44:22). 'As far as the east is from the west so far hath he removed our transgressions from us' (Psalm 103:12).

But it is precisely at this point that we taste defeat. We know these promises and many more. We believe them for they are there in the Word of God. But we find we cannot lay hold on them for ourselves. They are in our heads but they do not burn in our hearts as God's word to us. What then are we to do? Surely we must think back to the beginning of the Christian life and ask where faith comes from? Was it a special effort on our part that we first trusted in Christ? Of course not! Saving faith is the gift of God. But is this not still true? The faith by which the Christian receives God's Word is still and always will be a gift. So it is not a case of making a new effort to apply these promises. It is rather a question of crying to God that He will grant us by the working of the Spirit the faith to lay hold on the promises and to apply them to ourselves. It is the cry of the man in the gospel, 'Lord I believe, help thou mine unbelief'.

It was after penning some of the Psalms which have brought blessing to innumerable believers that David sinned so grievously. It was after his great confession at Caesarea Philippi that Simon Peter denied the Lord. But in neither case did they dwell on the past and wallow helplessly in the shame of failure. They came in repentance, and having found forgiveness they set their face to the future. If you are beset by some failure of the past go and read Psalm 51 and see David looking forward to such a complete restoration that he will teach transgressors God's ways. Go and look at Peter preaching on the day of Pentecost with his eyes on the tasks to which he is now committed. And when

Satán comes to accuse you, fling his charges in his face. Tell him Jesus has died. Take the sword of God's word and let every promise be a sword thrust to thwart the enemy and to repel him.

Later years

As the 'sixties passed, Mr Macfarlane's strength steadily declined. But many people remember his prayer meeting addresses from this period with a special warmth. He seemed to be particularly happy and relaxed at these meetings. He was soon unfit to take two services on the Lord's Day, however. He preached only once, either at Dingwall or at Beauly.

In the spring of 1973, about the time of Mr Macfarlane's eighty-fourth birthday, he became seriously ill. He did recover sufficiently to preach a number of times, but as the year wore on it became clear that he was now unable to carry on his work. It was a difficult decision for him to make, but in August of that year the link between a devoted pastor and a loving congregation was formally dissolved. Thus ended a fruitful ministry in Ross-shire — a ministry of forty-three years during which souls had been born again, believers built up in the faith, and young men and women called to serve the Lord in different parts of the world.

It was inevitable that his fifty-nine years in the ministry should come under appreciative review. But how deeply Mr Macfarlane felt his unworthiness was seen at that meeting of the Northern Presbytery at which his resignation was regretfully received.

The Moderator of the Presbytery, Rev. R. R. Sinclair, Wick, made a reference to Mr Macfarlane during the prayer with which the meeting was opened. When the time came for Mr Macfarlane to tender his resignation he said to the Moderator:

'I wish to thank you for your kind gospel spirit, which you showed in your opening prayer. It touched me deeply, and I don't think I'll forget it to the end of my days.

'I hope I am united to the one above, and to the brethren here — all of grace, of course; not for anything that is in here (pointing to himself). What is in here is a dung hill. Isn't that right?'

The other ministers on the Presbytery joined in paying tribute to Mr Macfarlane, but it was obvious that he had looked for none of this. In the car coming home from that meeting he said to his driver, 'Oh, well, they were very nice. And no one found any fault!' It was his shortcomings which were in his thoughts that day, and he was genuinely thankful that no one else had drawn attention to them.

As many have precious memories of these prayer meetings in Dingwall in the 'sixties, so many have similarly warm memories of visits to Mr Macfarlane's home in Inverness between 1973 and 1979. Relieved of his pastoral and preaching responsibilities, he was able to relax as he had not been able to do till then. And as different people went in the door of 2 Union Road, it was still the old Mr Macfarlane whom they found — with the same theological sharpness, the same gracious interest in everybody, the same humility and power in prayer.

As his strength decreased, his doctor would sometimes warn him not to read too much. But Mr Macfarlane had been given this advice by his doctor before, in Dingwall, and his comment then had been: 'For him to tell me to stop reading — it's as well for him to tell me not to take my food!'

This source of spiritual nourishment he refused to give up, almost to the end. Just months before he died, when he was ninety years old and physically weak, his wife came back from shopping to find him strengthened by a joy which was of God. He had been reading from the Epistles of John in Greek, and had greatly enjoyed the fresh thoughts which this had been bringing to his mind.

The triumph of grace

A particular aspect of these closing days of Mr Macfarlane's life was how, as bodily weakness advanced, he seemed to be increasingly 'strengthened by his Spirit in the inner man'. He still retained that acute sense of his sinfulness, that deep awareness of his need to be daily purged from sin. But along with this there was a growing confidence,

an increasing willingness to use the language of assurance.
He was being raised above his own natural tendency to
introspection, and Satan was not now being allowed that
access to him which had been permitted in the past.

During his last months he was very fond of reading a
book of sermons by John Colquhoun of Leith. On the
Monday of the last week of his life he asked his wife to
read one of the sermons from this book on *Sanctification.*
He seemed to relish the closing section in a new way:

> Depravity dwells beside grace in every faculty and
> member, and as the one is irreconcilably opposite
> to the other, the one constantly struggles against the
> other. 'The flesh lusteth against the spirit, and the
> spirit against the flesh.' In the understanding of a
> sanctified soul, remaining darkness lusteth against
> the light, and eagerly desires the destruction of it;
> and the light ardently desires, and attempts, the
> removal of the darkness. Sometimes the one prevails,
> and sometimes the other. At one time, the Christian
> experiences a longing after more of the knowledge
> of Christ; and at another he feels not only indiffer-
> ence, but even a degree of reluctance seeking it. In
> the sanctified will, aversion to holiness lusts against
> aversion to sin, and aversion to sin against aversion
> to holiness. The propension to holiness lusts against
> the remaining inclination to sin. The one lusts against,
> that is vehemently opposes and strongly exerts itself
> to overcome, the other. That takes place also in the
> affections of the soul. In them love and enmity, spiri-
> tuality and carnality, order and disorder, hope and
> fear, desire and aversion, constantly oppose and war
> against each other. 'What would ye see in the
> Shulamite? The company of two armies.' In so far as
> the believer is deserted, he acts according to the one
> principle; and so far as he is visited with renewed
> supplies of grace, he exerts himself according to the
> other. While sanctifying grace urges him forward to-
> ward the perfection of holiness, remaining depravity
> exerts itself to drag him back: while by the one he
> mounts up and soars aloft; by the other he is weighed

down, as to complain, 'My soul cleaveth to the dust'. The one principle counteracts the other in its activity, so that neither of them can carry their respective actings to perfection. 'That which I do,' says Paul, 'I allow not; for what I would, that do I not; but what I hate, that do I.' In proportion as the work of sanctification advances, remaining depravity, though weakened, will exert itself the more violently, and vex the believer the more keenly; nay, in some cases, prevail against him the more frequently: the struggle will become more vehement, and more harassing. But grace will finally overcome. Spiritual death will be swallowed up in victory.

Mr Macfarlane similarly appreciated another sermon from the same book, on *Union with Christ*; he asked his wife to read and re-read it to him during these last days. In the second part of that sermon Colquhoun speaks of the nature and properties of the believer's union with Christ, and the last point he makes is:

It is an *indissolvable* union. It is infinitely strong and durable. The saint shall be separated from his nearest relations, from his most intimate friends, from his dearest earthly enjoyments, and his soul ere long shall be separated from his body; but it shall never for a moment be parted from the Lord Jesus. Supposing the believer's body were burned, and every particle of its ashes removed as far from each other as the east is from the west, they would still be united, indissolvably united, to Jesus Christ; Romans 8:35–39. As death did not dissolve the hypostatical union in the person of Christ, so neither will it ever dissolve the mystical union between him and his saints. Their bodies when dissolved in the grave are as intimately united to the Lord Jesus as their souls dwelling in the mansions of glory. They sleep in Jesus: he keepeth all their bones. This union can never be dissolved; no creature can dissolve it, and the Lord Jesus himself will not. The creature cannot do it, 'Neither shall any man pluck them out of my hand.' He, the compassionate

Redeemer, will not. 'He will not turn away from them
to do them good.' Oh the safety, and honour and glory
of the true believer! His union with Christ shall continue
throughout all eternity.

Whatever distress and darkness he had come through in
the past, Mr Macfarlane was now able to rejoice in the union
between himself and Christ. He used to repeat that word
'indissolvable' with great emphasis — as also the word 'in-
violable', used by Colquhoun in the same connection. On
the indissolvability and inviolability of the union between
himself and Christ he rested, and in testimony of this he
said to a visitor during the last week of his life, 'I am going
to a better country'.

Afterwards, seeking to express her impressions of these
scenes, Mrs Macfarlane said: 'My memory of that last week
is of witnessing the struggle referred to in that sermon by
Colquhoun and of sharing with Donald in it. When he passed
away I had a sense of relief, of joy, of victory. I rejoiced for
him that the conflict had been for ever resolved in the
triumph of grace in glory.'

Mr. Macfarlane, taken in Glasgow on the day of his first wedding, August 1928.

2.
Personal appreciation by
J. Cameron Fraser

As mentioned in the biographical sketch, Mr Mac-
farlane married for the second time in 1957. His
second wife, Ella Finlayson, was Cameron Fraser's
aunt. This relationship became particularly signifi-
cant because Cameron, whose father had died in
1959, was bereaved also of his mother in 1961.
Thus at the age of six years he went, along with
his two older sisters, to stay with his Aunt Ella
in the Dingwall manse.

(Cameron Fraser is the son of James Fraser,
the story of whose missionary work in Zimbabwe
is told in the book **James Fraser,** *published by*
the Banner of Truth Trust.)

The day before he passed away, my uncle bade farewell to
his wife and a nursing friend of the family. In a voice which
by now was barely audible he said, 'I want to be with Jesus,
I want to be like Jesus. I want you all to be like Jesus.'
When he said that, Mr Macfarlane was not only giving
expression to the dying wish of a mature Christian; he
was articulating what had been for him the controlling
influence of his entire ministry, from early manhood to
this his 90th year.

It was a great privilege to grow up from childhood to
adulthood in the home and under the influence of a man
generally regarded by those who knew him as a spiritual
and intellectual giant without an equal in his immediate
ecclesiastical fellowship. Indeed, it would be difficult to
find men anywhere with a deeper understanding of spiritual
truth, combined with such a self effacing humility and
utter devotion to the Person of the Lord Jesus Christ. To

have grown up with such company and under such an
influence was indeed a rare blessing, and it is out of a desire
to express my gratitude to God for it that I am writing this
personal appreciation of my late uncle.

As I look back on those years, several things stand out.
First, there was my uncle's massive learning and phenomenal
memory, coupled with a genuine sense of personal unworthiness. For example, despite his obvious qualifications to act
as a theological tutor, he seemed genuinely unconscious of
his own abilities. I remember him telling me that he had
been asked to tutor for a few years until more able men were
raised up! This was honestly how he understood the
situation.

My uncle's academic interests ranged far beyond theological disciplines as such, and he taught himself such subjects as psychology, which he thought would be helpful to
him in the ministry. He used to stress the importance of
studying philosophy, particularly if one had the ministry
in mind. In such cases, he also encouraged mastery of the
biblical languages and was distressed by those who did not
share his enthusiasm for a rigorous academic preparation
for the ministry. At the same time, he was most understanding of those less gifted than himself, and there surely could
not have been a more lenient examination marker! Mr
Macfarlane always regretted the fact that lack of funds
prevented him from studying for the honours degree at
Aberdeen. I once asked him if he thought that such further
studies would have been as useful as the practical experience
he had gained in the ministry. His reply was 'Ten times
more useful!'

A second feature of the man I came to know as my uncle
was his consistent graciousness. He was a gentleman almost
to a fault.

His graciousness was particularly evident in his relations
with ministerial brethren, both within and beyond his
denominational fellowship. Whatever differences he might
have with them on certain issues, he never allowed this to
colour his personal relationships with them. He remained
throughout his life committed to the separate existence
of the Free Presbyterian Church. Yet his loyalty to the
Church never deteriorated into a party spirit and, in the
biblical sense of the word, his outlook was truly ecumenical.

In his later years my uncle was considerably encouraged by a renewal of Reformed teaching among young ministers in the Church of Scotland, and he followed this development with deep interest.

Undergirding the above characteristics, there was my uncle's deep spirituality and almost total absorption in the things of God. No one could come into contact with him for any length of time without being made aware of this. His prayers were exceptional in the warmth of their devotion and the immediate yet reverend sense of the divine presence which they expressed. Dr Edmund P. Clowney, then President of Westminster Theological Seminary, who met my uncle briefly while on a visit to Scotland, spoke afterwards of the beautiful blessing which my uncle had 'pronounced' on him and his work. In prayer his language was suffused with Scripture. He did not seem to be quoting scripture directly; rather his vocabulary was formed by Scripture.

He disliked the popular highland practice of 'spiritualising' Old Testament passages with little or no regard to their historical context and immediate meaning. He was always careful himself to do justice to the background of a text, and to place it in its proper setting in the flow of redemptive history. Preaching he defined as 'textual and contextual exegesis', adding that it was questionable whether anything not fitting that definition should be called 'preaching'.

At times my uncle could be plagued by doubts and fears arising out of his profound sense of personal unworthiness. Psalm 130 was particularly helpful on one such occasion and I Corinthians 1:30,31 was a favourite passage. He also received help from writers such as John Owen (especially volume 3 of Owen's *Works*). Halyburton was another author whom he often quoted and recommended. Guthrie's *Trial of a Saving Interest* and Calamy's *The Godly man's Ark* were also helpful in times of need.

He possessed an extensive library of theological books, each one of which was heavily underlined and marked, the result of having been read and re-read many times. His sets of Owen's *Works* and Calvin's *Institutes* were particularly dog-eared to the point of falling apart. During his last days, he particularly enjoyed a rare, tattered book of Sermons by John Colquhoun of Leith. When he was unable to read

himself, my aunt would read this work to him and it seemed
to draw them even closer together and at the same time
prepare them both for the inevitable separation that lay
ahead.

After I left Scotland to study at Westminster Theological
Seminary in Philadelphia, I was able to make annual visits
home in the summer time. At the end of one of those visits
in 1978 (at which time I introduced my future wife) I prayed
that we might all meet again in this world. In the good
providence of God that prayer was answered. I was able to
make a short trip in October of 1979, arriving on the 24th —
the day before my uncle passed away. I had known that
his health was deteriorating but did not expect the end to
be so close. To witness his departure to be with the Lord
was an unforgettable privilege. The entire experience was
a very practical lesson in the fact that God gives promised
grace in times of need. As we anticipated the inevitable we
dreaded it, but in the hour of death we were all conscious
of a peace that passes understanding. That is surely how my
uncle would have wished to leave us.

3.
An appreciation by the editor

My mother's father was an elder in Mr Macfarlane's congregation of Dingwall and Beauly. It was while under Mr Macfarlane's pastoral care that my mother became a communicant member in the church, before she left to marry my father in 1933.

I have a few memories of Mr Macfarlane from the 'fifties. (Our home was then in Stornoway, but we used to go for our summer holidays to Dingwall, where my grandmother and my aunt were living).

The first part of the following incident I do not remember. But my mother tells me that she, along with my brother and I and a number of other people, were in a home belonging to Mr Macfarlane's congregation. My mother remembers vividly how Mr Macfarlane, in the course of a prayer which was tender and yet powerful, came to pray especially for the young people present and to use the petition which Jacob pled in his old age for his grandchildren: 'The Angel which redeemed me from all evil bless the lads' (Genesis 48:16).

What I remember about that day was that Mr Macfarlane gave my brother Cameron and me a lift back to our grandmother's home. His old Morris Minor sailed along, and his arms were all over the place. He was pointing to cattle in fields which we were passing, or to a man whom he thought we should know, and at least once we had to come to a very sudden halt. Previously, Cameron and I had assumed that a driver needed to look at the road in order to keep on it. We found it intriguing that Mr Macfarlane seemed to live above this requirement!

When my father died in 1960, my mother decided to leave

Stornoway for Dingwall in order to be near my grandmother
and my aunt. It was difficult to part with friends who were
warm and spiritual; so it was with many backward looks that
I came to Dingwall in July of that year. It was not easy then
to think of the privilege which this move to Dingwall was to
bring. However, as time passed, the uniqueness of the
privilege began to dawn. No doubt Mr Macfarlane could
not offer that type of warmth and intimacy which I was
missing. But he had greater depth.

My mother had professed faith in Christ when Mr Macfarlane's ministry in Dingwall had been just beginning. So
now my brother Cameron and I did, as the same ministry
was entering its final phase. Looking back on these years
of great privilege, what can one say about Mr Macfarlane's
personality, his preaching and his pastoral influence?

His personality

It will have already become clear that Mr Macfarlane's
personality was unusual. He was not without a sense of
humour. When he was about to accompany me as a divinity
student into the pulpit (he would get almost *anyone* to
preach instead of himself) he would unfailingly say 'Now
you'll ask Mr Grant to pray, as he's *older*.' At that stage
Mr Macfarlane would be about eighty years old and Mr
Grant (a retired minister in the congregation) eighty-two;
and when Mr Macfarlane used this argument to have himself excused there would be a real twinkle in his eye.

But the overall impression from Mr Macfarlane was one
of seriousness. Probably he was retiring to a fault, and the
church suffered because of his unwillingness to recognise
the extraordinary gifts God had given him. And yet, out
of the anguish of self-doubt which Mr Macfarlane at times
experienced, there was born a sympathy towards others
in trouble and an understanding of the difficulties through
which they were called to pass. Surely this is part of the
reason why he was the opposite of harsh and censorious.
He was tender when dealing with the failings of God's
people; and when denouncing sin he had such a compassionate spirit towards the sinner that his denunciations had

double effect. It was an illustration of McCheyne's words: 'A holy minister is an awful weapon in the hands of God'.

And another point — did Mr Macfarlane's self-doubt not indirectly contribute to his excelling in study? He had a dread of resting in anything superficial in his own relationship with God, and he was afraid of offering anything insubstantial to others. He had such high standards, and such a low estimate of his own attainments, that he drove himself to study spiritual and theological issues with a rigour even greater than would otherwise have been the case.

His preaching

Mr Macfarlane liked to get a subject for preaching a week, or even more, beforehand. He studied the text and context thoroughly, writing pages of compressed notes. After that he would sit back in the chair that was before his study fire and close his eyes. He had usually finished sermon preparation before Saturday. On the morning of the Lord's Day he would get up early, go down to his study and would again prayerfully go over the material he had prepared. About an hour before going out to preach he would gather up the notes he had been going over and burn them in the fire.

There was a certain informality about Mr Macfarlane's preaching — both in his manner, and in his way of presenting his subject. The main elements were clearly before his mind, but he liked to feel free as to how he would develop and present a point. And it was amazing at times to see how he could take up options as he felt inclined, and explore them. He seemed to be completely at home, wherever in Scripture he might want to go. I remember his once taking up the false priests referred to in the Book of Jeremiah as an illustration of how the general benevolence of God still extended to those who are not embraced within his special love. It seemed that, wherever his mind turned in the Prophecy, whole sections of it opened up before his mind. Within a few minutes he had worked together details from the visions, the prophecies, and the biographical sections to illustrate his point.

His having such an informed and fertile mind obviously had its dangers. It was possible for him to become so involved in something that opened up to him at a particular point that his hearers got lost. They might forget what the main point was, or might be unable to grasp the relevance of the subsidiary point. Unusual theological questions would attract him (and he would find it difficult to tear himself away!) For example, he once said in the course of a sermon, in the manner of an aside, 'I would like to think that it will be a subject for the meditation of the saints in glory — the relationship between the Holy Spirit and the human nature of Christ while he was in the world.'

Although there was an absence of stuffy formality, there came over in his preaching a sense of how solemn he felt it for himself and his hearers to be under the scrutiny of God's word. He was not there to put on a show or to pass the time. His great desire was that both he and his congregation would be led by the Holy Spirit into the word of God.

It seemed to me that, in his preaching, he had three principal aims. He wanted to lay bare the main points in his text, he wanted to show how they related to the way of salvation revealed in the whole of Scripture, and he wanted to show their relevance and application to himself and his hearers.

In grappling with the essential teaching of a text, obviously he was at an advantage with his exceptional knowledge of the original languages. Not that he ever made a display of his knowledge. Sometimes his understanding of a Hebrew idiom would be crucial to his explanation of a text, but the congregation would not be made aware that Hebrew had anything to do with it.

He was continually wrestling with the form in which the truth was expressed, in order to show his hearers the substance of it. He would take Old Testament ritual and place it in a New Testament setting; he would take the language of the New Testament and put it in the mouths of Old Testament saints. He would do almost anything to bring people face to face with the abiding, central doctrines of the Scriptures. He used to paraphrase the Shorter Catechism, too, with the same purpose. Speaking once about the Ark of the Covenant, and how the gold represented

Christ's divine nature and the wood his human nature, he called on the Shorter Catechism, Question 21, to help him.

Q. 'Who is the redeemer of God's elect?

A. 'The only redeemer of God's elect is the Lord Jesus Christ, who being from all eternity gold, became acacia wood, and so was and continueth to be gold and acacia wood, in two distinct natures, and one person, for ever.' For him, it was not enough simply to quote from the *Confession of Faith* — presenting its doctrines as truths which had been arranged by the church in a fixed form. In his hands, the life which is in the various doctrines of the faith shone through the forms in which they found expression.

He would approach an aspect of Christian experience from different points of view. He loved to show, for example, that the faith of Old Testament saints was essentially the same as that of New Testament believers, though the revelation to which that faith looked came to fuller expression in New Testament times. He also liked to approach doctrines from different angles, and particularly to show how one doctrine implies and leads into another. In this way, although his sermons lacked the usual signs of order, they were often characterised by unity and wholeness at a deep level.

Apart from his theological learning, his exigetical skill and his spiritual insight, another outstanding aspect of Mr Macfarlane as a preacher was his imagination. It came to him in a completely natural way to reconstruct a Scriptural scene, sometimes putting words into a character's mouth which would indicate vividly what his thoughts must have been. He would also use metaphors which he worked out with extraordinary imaginative power. Sometimes there would be a tension between the sublimity of the subject and the earthiness of the illustration which, at least for some hearers, served to heighten the effect.

His pastoral influence

Many people felt that Mr Macfarlane's prayers were perhaps the most outstanding aspect of his ministry. If you succeeded in persuading him to pray after you had preached, the

experience was a humbling, though also an uplifting one.
You saw the superficiality of your own thought and feeling,
compared to his. He did not know that this was going on,
but the fact that his thoughts were deeper and his language
richer could not be concealed. His language was so unusual,
but it was natural to him; and at a pace that was unforced
for him he would cover more ground in a short prayer
than most of us could in a whole sermon. His prayers were
attended with great solemnity; but they were offered, too,
in an atmosphere of unusual intimacy and ease. He would
pray for particular issues and particular people in a way
that could not fail to warm one's heart. I remember how
his pastor's prayerful concern for his people showed itself
at the end of a long communion service on a Sabbath morning in Beauly church. Perhaps others were only thinking of
what a happy privilege it had been for them to be there.
But Mr Macfarlane was thinking about an elderly man belonging to the congregation who was at that time in the Dingwall
hospital. So part of the prayer with which the service was
concluded went:

> Bless the weak, the sick, the dying. Grant that there
> be not a veil, a thick partition, between their hearts
> and Christ; but that they get a home in him for eternity.
> Bless thy dear children here. Give them a drink, a
> long drink of Christ. They desire, as it were, to take
> their heart and place it in the hollow of Christ's hand.
> *Be with John Livingstone today, in hospital in Ding-*
> *wall.* Grant to draw near to him as thou didst draw near
> to the two on the way to Emmaus — and then he will
> not be lonely, and he will not feel the time long.

On another occasion when Mr Macfarlane prayed for someone who was ill in hospital, the person concerned was not a
member of his own congregation. He was the headmaster
of Dingwall Academy — an exceptionally conscientious
man, who had done a lot for generations of pupils. We
who were then pupils in the school were particularly struck
by how Mr Macfarlane made one mid-week service at the
time into a prayer meeting so that those who prayed could
remember the headmaster in a special way. However, Mr

Macfarlane's request, at least during the earlier part of the prayer meeting, went more or less unheeded; and when he reminded us of it he seemed to me to show just a little of the frustration expressed in the *Diary of Kenneth Macrae:*

> On Thursday we had a Day of Humiliation and Prayer appointed by the presbytery . . . Conducted it purely as a prayer meeting . . . One of the prayers was inordinately long, inarticulately uttered, and, so far as I could understand, had no bearing on the matter which brought us together. A simple, direct little prayer would be far more to the point than a volume of divinity. These long, wordy, wandering prayers one hears so often in these quarters nowadays are squeezing the life out of our prayer meetings.
> (*Diary of Kenneth Macrae*, Banner of Truth Trust, page 386)

One of the times when visitors to the congregation were struck by Mr Macfarlane's stature as a pastor was when he conducted an adult baptism just a few years before he retired. It was at the Friday evening service of a Communion Season in Dingwall and there was a large congregation. When the normal service was over, conducted by another minister, the pulpit door opened and Mr Macfarlane made his way down the pulpit steps. An eighteen-year-old Dutch girl rose near the front and came forward. The two of them stood there in front of the pulpit, and Mr Macfarlane explained the significance of baptism and spoke about the girl's desire to profess her Lord. He referred to opportunities which would arise for her to serve him, and to how she should prayerfully make use of these. He was speaking so tenderly, as one on the same level as this young convert. He was eighty and she was eighteen; and yet it seemed that all barriers were at that moment taken down and those words were really fulfilled: 'Ye are all one in Christ Jesus'. There was such peace, there was such gospel unity, that I remember feeling, before the end of that service, 'If heaven has anything like the atmosphere in the church tonight, I would like to be there.'

Many memories stand out from the period after Mr Macfarlane
retired to Inverness. One illustrates the kind of conversation
which only Mr Macfarlane could provide. Another minister
had been in for tea, and as he was leaving a lively spiritual
exchange took place between this minister and Mr Macfarlane:

> *D. A. Macf.* 'Oh well, we need the ground cut clean
> away from beneath our feet, so that we'll
> fall holus bolus into the covenant of
> grace — is that right?'
> *W. M.* 'Oh yes, yes; but we'll be cleaving to the
> covenant of works!'
> *D. A. Macf.* 'Yes! Cleaving with our teeth — teeth
> that we haven't got!'

Another illustrates how practical his Christianity was.
My wife and I called at Union Road while going off on
holiday, and he insisted on giving us some money to help
with the cost of petrol. Remonstrations were of no avail;
the matter was closed with the words, 'You see, I am too
old to go on holiday, and you'll do instead.' I felt that, if
I had ever seen a person's own interests lost in those of
another, it was then.

My last memory of him is from a hurried visit fitted into
that day when we left Kinlochbervie, my first charge, to
come to Aberdeen. It was a difficult day — physically,
emotionally and spiritually. But most of the details I have
forgotten, except those five minutes standing at his bed-
side. He was very weak, and his voice indistinct, but he was
speaking about the keeper of Israel who never says 'I am
feeling very heavy; I will need to take a rest for a while'.

Five minutes of peace in a troubled day. Does that not
represent what Mr Macfarlane's ministry often meant to
those whom it embraced?

Part Two

1964: In the garden of the Dingwall manse, with his wife Ella and two of her nephews. The older is J. Cameron Fraser (see page 37).

4.
Sermons

Editorial note

The material which appears in the following pages was derived from a variety of sources. Some sermons were sent by Mr Macfarlane himself to the Church Magazine. But there were very few of these, and in any case they largely lacked that naturalness and power which often characterised his preached sermons. Other sermons were taken down in shorthand, from as far back as the 1930's. Then there were little quotes, like the one about the *S.S. SALVATION,* which I found in my grandmother's writing in an old note book. But the majority of the material came from notes which my mother made in long hand, during the last thirteen years of Mr Macfarlane's ministry.

Mr Macfarlane was very emphatic that he did not go into the pulpit with an address which was ready for printing. He felt that it was an essential aspect of his approach to preaching that he should feel free to present his message in an informal, almost conversational, way. It was partly for this reason that he was extremely sensitive, at least for most of his ministry, about any record of his sermons being made, either by note-taking or by the use of a tape recorder. This is one reason why, in the preparation of this book, a large degree of editing has been carried out.

Another reason is this. For those who were used to hearing him preach, it might have been preferable to print more of his sermons in the form in which he presented them. But what about those for whom these pages are to provide their first encounter with his ministry? Differences of spiritual background and of language might have combined with Mr Macfarlane's own particular unusualness to keep the encounter from proving really profitable.

51

The editing, then, will perhaps involve a loss to some. But I hope it will mean that a wider public will be better placed to benefit from a ministry which, while in some respects unique, derived its greatest strengths from those essential elements of the gospel which are the salvation and the glory of the whole united church of Christ.

A gift to mark a new age

To you . . . a Saviour
Luke 2:11

The Saviour

We read at the beginning of this chapter of the Roman enrol-
ment because of which Joseph went up to Bethlehem to be
taxed with Mary, his espoused wife, who was in a state of
motherhood at this time. Joseph and Mary sought shelter
and comfort in the inn, but there was no room for them
there. On this night 'that holy thing' which was to be called
'the Son of God' was born in the stable. Mary wrapped him
in swaddling clothes and laid him in a manger. Here, then,
was the first holy, harmless and undefiled being who was
ever found among men from the fall of Adam. (Perhaps we
may regard that as showing that he was holy in relation to
the Father, harmless in relation to men, and undefiled as to
his own holy heart.) Nor will there be such a being again
born of the human family. Here was a clean thing brought
out of an unclean — separate from sinners, yet truly human.
Here we have one who was all that man ought to be, yet
superhuman in his divine conception.

God did not prepare a body for the Saviour as he did
for the first Adam. He formed man of the dust of the
earth. He breathed into his nostrils the breath of life, and
man became a living soul. But a body was not formed for
the Saviour apart from the human family. Otherwise we may
say that the Saviour would be apart from them, outwith the
family, though like them as man.

He came into the family without sin; yet he came under the law. 'Forasmuch then as the children were partakers of flesh and blood, he also himself likewise took part of the same, that through death he might destroy him that had the power of death, that is the devil; and deliver them who through fear of death were all their lifetime subject to bondage' (Hebrews 2:14—15). The long-promised Messiah had at length come. Mary and Joseph handled and cared with sanctified affection for the 'Truth' of Abraham and the 'Mercy' of Jacob, for the child born in the city of David was exactly the realisation of that 'truth' and 'mercy'. They had the Heir to the throne of his father David in their arms. 'He shall reign over the house of David for ever, and of his kingdom there shall be no end.'

In the midst of outward lowliness and need, the Most High manifested nevertheless the glory of him who 'humbled himself, and was found in fashion as a man.' What a difference between lowly circumstances, and even dire poverty, on the one hand, and sin on the other! Poverty is despised by the natural man, where and when he has some fair measure of worldly goods. But, as the Redeemer was not ashamed of the cross, so he was not ashamed in his infinite condescending love, burning in holy jealousy as a fire, to take to himself a true body, and a reasonable soul, being conceived by the power of the Holy Ghost in the womb of the Virgin Mary, and born of her, *in this stable,* yet without sin. 'Foxes have holes, and the birds of the air have nests, but the Son of Man hath not where to lay his head.'

The shepherds

The glory of the risen Sun of Righteousness in his divine dignity of eternal sonship was immediately to be made known to these shepherds, and they, being dead, yet speak to us. They were abiding in the fields, watching over their flocks by night. These men were witnesses 'before ordained of God' to witness to the birth of the child Jesus. Were they already like-minded with Joseph, Mary, Zacharias, Elizabeth, Simeon, Anna and others, waiting for the

'Consolation of Israel'? While it is not definitely asserted, there is much reason to conclude that they were — and if so, 'Blessed are they who have not seen and yet have believed'. Certainly we believe that they were so blessed when they went to the manger, and later on when they took up the celestial song of the heavenly host and published it to the cities of Judah, saying, 'Behold your God!'

In the midst of the quietness and stillness of the night as they, perhaps by turns, snatched moments of sleep and waited for the morning, suddenly the angel of the Lord appeared to them, and the glory of the Lord shone round about them. They were sore afraid. What a lesson is here, to show how men at the Great Day shall be terror stricken! Who can conceive what the glory, majesty and power revealed at the Second Coming of the Saviour will be like!

The angel comforted them, allayed their fears, and proceeded to declare to them his message. 'Fear not; for, behold, I bring you good tidings of great joy, which shall be to all people. For unto you is born this day in the City of David a Saviour, which is Christ the Lord.' Along with the revelation was a sign given of where they would find the babe — and on that there broke out the song of the heavenly host, glorifying and praising God. What a scene, and what a meeting! A short time previously all was quietness and the ear quick to hear any disturbance among the flocks — any prowling jackal or sheep-stealer — now this gospel message, followed by a song of the celestial Zion. This was a hallowed meeting, a sanctifying revelation when accompanied by the blessing of the Holy Spirit. They believed the tidings about the Saviour. They came and saw everything as it had been told them, and they returned glorifying and praising God for all the things which had been shown to them.

The song

We may here briefly observe what is revealed in the song of the host. The birth of the Saviour gave glory to God in the highest. The reason for that special glory redounding to God was that thereby peace was on earth — and that peace flowed from the good will of God to men. Good will, or as the Shorter Catechism tells us, 'mere good pleasure',

or sovereign grace, is the eternal origin of peace on earth.
Apart from that, there is no good will among men toward
God. Wherever there is any good will, as among the godly,
they know and own that it is due to God giving his Christ
as the gift of his good will to a lost world.

At New Year friends send gifts to one another. In some
cases these gifts are as 'a friend in need, a friend indeed'.
In other cases they are an expression of affection and remembrance. There would, however, be no New Year for a dismal,
dark world, sitting in the shadow of death, were it not for
Christ. He brings a new era into the world — gives a New
Year, a new beginning, a new spiritual abiding peace, a new
life, a new eternity where there is no more sorrow nor
sighing for the former things are passed away. And Christ
the Lord is the Father's present, not to friends, but to foes.
He still says to us, 'Unto you is a Saviour — the anointed
king over the house of David for ever; and of his kingdom
there shall be no end.' He says, as it were, to us 'He is yours
in my gracious offer; take him. He is my peace to you, he
is my good-will gift to you. I do not spare him. I love them
who love him, and those who seek him early shall find him
and me.' Christ is the Peace of the earth, for shepherds in
Judea, and for 'all people'. He is the essence of willingness
to give the needy penitent soul peace with the Father, with
divine justice, with the Law in its command and holy
penalty, a peace of conscience that, although our sins are as
scarlet, he can so wash as to make us sweet, clean, healthy
and send the soul who boasts in him away with this song,
'Glory to God in the heavenly places in Christ Jesus!' He
sends the poor away filled with good things. If a needy soul
is enabled, through victory over self and by a divine melting, to rest with heart and soul on Christ as his Saviour,
then the inhabitants in glory hear of it in the streets of the
City of David above. They rejoice that another soul has had
his tongue unloosed and has joined the ransomed of the
Lord who are returning to Zion with songs and everlasting
joy on their heads.

Is your face towards Zion, or are you going the other
way? What is the root-cause if a soul in a gospel land is not
learning this song? The cause is pride of heart. Our pride is
deeper, greater than we realise. Our pride hinders our stoop-

ing, our taking to heart our guilt, misery, our lost estate.
And if we are 'whole', we cannot prize the Physician. He
gives peace, not in sin but through salvation from sin. May
we be enabled and willing to detect sin, to perceive its
workings and lurkings, and be in dispeace with it, crying
to him to work in us habitually to 'will and to do of his
good pleasure'.

But to conclude our remarks. They went, they saw.
They returned glorifying God. Who took care of their
flocks when they went to Bethlehem? Why ask? What did
they need to care though they were all stolen, when they
were so blessed? They counted all but loss to win Christ.
Earthly cares were left upon the Lord; and the Shepherd
who cared for their souls cared for their flocks. What a
gospel day they enjoyed in the watches of that night! 'If
I say, Surely the darkness shall cover me; even the night
shall be light about me. Yea, the darkness hideth not from
thee, but the night shineth as day; the darkness and the
light are both alike to thee.'

We take leave of the shepherds on these Delectable
Mountains — Mount Great Joy, Mount Peace, Mount Good-
will, Mount Glory. We hear no more of the shepherds.
They published abroad what they saw and heard. The Day
will declare who heard and became restless until they also
saw the sanctifying secret of the gospel. They are long
gone to their Father's house. They are of one mind and
in the one place. They are still being holily refreshed with
the presence of, and enjoying holy communion with, him
who is the 'Truth' of Abraham, the 'Mercy' of Jacob, the
'Peace' of God, the manifestation of his 'Goodwill' to all
who flee to his wings' shade. They are holily satisfied and
yet for ever receiving out of his fulness, or as Owen likes
to put it, 'full and being filled,' for 'to him that hath shall
be given, and he shall have more abundantly.'

Which of these two parties, do you think — these worthy
shepherds or the 'heavenly host' — knows more of that
heavenly song, 'Glory to God in the highest'? We may leave
it that the shepherds are glad that they ever heard it sung
outside Bethlehem; and the heavenly host rejoices with
joy unspeakable that the shepherds were made able and
willing to know it experimentally and to sing it here below
to the praise of God's glorious grace.

Christ preaching at Nazareth

The Spirit of the Lord is upon me, because he hath anointed me to preach the gospel to the poor; he hath sent me to heal the brokenhearted, to preach deliverance to the captives, and recovering of sight to the blind, to set at liberty them that are bruised.

Luke 4:18

Here, the Lord of Glory reads his own commission to preach the gospel to the poor, to heal the brokenhearted, to preach deliverance to the captives, and recovering of sight to the blind, to set at liberty them that are bruised. No remedy would be of any avail for those who are poor in this sense, except the Redeemer and his fullness, and all that his person embraces in his humiliation and exhaltation. 'Neither is there salvation in any other, for there is none other name under heaven given among men whereby we must be saved.'

In what sense are those poor to whom Christ was anointed to preach the gospel? They are poor in their consciences. They are so poor that nothing will relieve their poverty but Christ and his gospel applied by the Holy Spirit, leading sinners into the infinitely excellent salvation of the Redeemer. They are brought in measure to see that they are poor, poor, poor, because they lack the substance of John 17:3, 'And this is life eternal, that they might know thee the only living and true God, and Jesus Christ whom thou hast sent.' Until we come to know and to receive the Redeemer, we are in a state of spiritual poverty; and even after being united to him we feel that, while rich in him, we are in ourselves poor and needy, needing him more and more through time and eternity.

58

Our will also is in a state of poverty, until we are made submissive to the King of Sion in the gospel. We shall never come to this, unless secretly made willing by the Holy Spirit. Let us take with us words and plead, 'Draw me, touch me, bring me out of my spiritual grave, make me a lowly debtor to the Redeemer.' Where that is, then it can be said, 'A willing people in thy day of power shall come to thee.' This is the day of spiritual resurrection, for saving grace is a spiritual resurrection in the will.

Those spoken of in our text are also poor in their affections. They have no holy love, fear, worship or adoration of the Lamb, and even when they do get a taste of this they mourn over their lack of love and of repentance — how few tears they have in God's bottle, how little they grasp of the Redeemer in the gospel.

He has anointed me. The Father gave the Son. 'If the blood of bulls and of goats, and the ashes of an heifer sprinkling the unclean, sanctifieth to the purifying of the flesh: how much more shall the blood of Christ, who through the eternal Spirit offered himself without spot to God, purge your conscience from dead works to serve the living God?' If the blood of Christ satisfies the justice of God, should it not satisfy you and me?

Those who heard him preach in Nazareth were laden with privileges; but they never got a view of the glory of Christ through the mirror of the promises. They were poor and wretched and miserable and blind and naked. But the devil in effect said to them, 'You are not poor at all. Jesus of Nazareth preaches the gospel to the poor, but this does not apply to you. He preaches the opening of the doors to the prisoners but not for you — you are free and going to heaven. The Lord is well pleased with you. Only the wicked Gentiles have need of that gospel.' Although they said, 'We have Abraham to our father,' they did not understand the Old Testament which told of the Redeemer who was to come. If they had not been proud and lifted up, they would have received the Redeemer and his sermon. They were sitting in judgment on him, instead of being poor and feeling their need of him. If they had had spiritual understanding of the truth, they would immediately have taken to the Redeemer and said like Nathaniel, 'Thou art

the Son of God; thou art the King of Israel.' How near they
were to the cup of salvation on the table of the gospel,
but they were in a state of carnal security, self wisdom,
good in their own eyes. And when the Saviour spoke of
the sovereignty of God and gave an example of the widow
of Sarepta as one whom the Lord raised up from among
the Gentiles, they would have cast the blessed Saviour
over the brow of the hill.

But suppose that, with those gathered to hear Christ when
he preached in the synagogue, there could be Abel, Enoch,
Abraham, Isaac and Jacob, Moses, Samuel and those that
called upon his name, David and Isaiah. We know that
they could not be taken back from Glory; but supposing
they were back in the tabernacle of the body, and they
were asked to be good enough to sit down and listen to
the sermon, with the secret unction of the Holy One, the
earnest of the promised inheritance, what would they have
said? They would have said, 'We do not need to see any
miracles performed on the blind and deaf to assure us that
this is the promised Messiah. He did miracles long ago for
us.' 'What do you say, David?' 'O, he gave me thousands
of miracles to put in the Psalms.' Isaiah would say, 'I wrote
these promises about preaching the gospel to the poor,
and not one of them was revealed without a spiritual
miracle, and they will be the means of more and more
miracles until the blast of the last trump. And now we
see him actually in the flesh of whom, through the Spirit,
I wrote so long ago.'
    Like Peter, and the other disciples around the Saviour,
Isaiah would say, 'Thou hast the words of eternal life'.
And when the sermon was concluded, Isaiah might say,
'This very sermon we got today is full and overflowing
with spiritual miracles. Here is the golden pot that had
manna, and here is the bright and morning star. I think
we should sing a few verses of Psalm 45 — what David saw
in advance by the Holy Spirit:

> *Thou fairer art than sons of men;*
>   *into thy lips is store*
> *Of grace infus'd . . .*

If you were to ask all these Old Testament saints, along with Peter, James and John, and all those about the Saviour who were his own sheep, 'Are you prepared to sing Psalm 89 in face of him today?' their answer would be 'By all means.

> *In vision to thy Holy One*
> *thou saidst, I help upon*
> *A strong one laid; out of the folk*
> *I rais'd a chosen one.*

Here is the strong one to deliver us from our badness, our unholiness, our coldness, our deadness. Although we are as unprofitable as we are, we desire to be like him, and to go to be with him.'

Nathanael

John 1:45—51

From the Saviour's words, 'Behold an Israelite indeed, in whom is no guile,' we can safely infer that Nathanael was a God-fearing man, though not that he was perfect. His desire was to be in harmony in mind and heart with the Holy Ghost, and to be consecrated to the service of the Most High. He may have been a gracious man for years before this meeting with Christ, or it may have been on that very day that he got spiritual enlightenment. The Redeemer knew what was in his heart; Nathaniel could have said with David, —

> *My footsteps and my lying down,*
> *thou compassest always;*
> *Thou also most entirely art*
> *acquaint with all my ways.*

Behold an Israelite indeed, and coming to me, desiring to be totally in harmony with the truth in love. He was steeped in the spirit of the godly under the Old Testament dispensation, and steeped in the spirit of holy love to the whole counsel of God, as far as he understood it. He had a measure of God-given entrance into the word of God as revealed under the Old Testament dispensation. Nathanael was of the same spirit as Abel who saw Christ in the first promise — that the seed of the woman would bruise the head of the serpent, or death, hell and Satan. He was to procure life for the soul and immortality for the body through the gospel. The first sacrifice was just a promise that the blood of Jesus Christ, God's Son, cleanses from all sin. If we do not believe in the blood of Christ and in the Christ of the blood, then we are frittering away our time this Sabbath evening. This is a holy, sanctifying as well as justifying truth. It is impossible to believe in the blood of sprinkling without beginning to love the Father and the Redeemer, and the salvation of the gospel.

'Come and see,' Philip had said to him; and all that Nathanael saw with his bodily eyes was Christ's human nature; but Nathanael discerned through the unction of the Holy One that he was indeed the Lord of Glory. 'Thou art the King of Israel, who was to come in the fullness of time.' Here we have grace reigning through righteousness unto eternal life.

When Nathanael said, 'Rabbi, thou art the Son of God, thou art the King of Israel,' we could almost say that he had passed into the New Testament dispensation. He was in the porch of it, on the very threshold of it. He had already seen Christ's day afar off, but now he got a further exercise of faith, building himself up in his most holy faith.

When Philip brought Nathanael to Christ, it was as if the Redeemer said, 'O my dove, that art in the clefts of the rock, let me see thy countenance, let me hear thy voice, for sweet is thy voice, and thy countenance is comely.' *Come along now, dove Nathanael, let me see thy countenance.* Nathanael manifested his countenance; were they not all seeing his countenance of soul? And if the stamp of the character of your soul were shown up could you say, like Peter, 'Lord, thou knowest all things, thou knowest that I love thee'? We believe that this would be the confession of Nathanael.

In verse 51 we have the promise: 'Hereafter ye shall see heaven opened, and the angels of God ascending and descending upon the Son of Man.' Probably this referred to the ascension. Note that it says first, 'ascending', which suggests that they were down already at his command. If it refers to the ascension, Nathanael was there and saw some of the angels there. We believe the angels of Glory went with the Redeemer:

God is with shouts gone up,
   The Lord with trumpets sounding high.
Sing praise to God, sing praise, sing praise.
   Praise to our King sing ye.

Nathanael is in Glory now, with the spirits of just men
made perfect, and sees and discerns that angels are, and
desire to be, consecrated to God. This is part of what he
enjoys — to know that the angels are ministering spirits
sent forth to minister to the heirs of salvation. Angels
carried the soul of Lazarus to Abraham's bosom, and it is
probable that they so minister to all the godly.

Deliverance from captivity

I will surely assemble, O Jacob, all of thee; I will surely gather the remnant of Israel; I will put them together as the sheep of Bozrah, as the flock in the midst of their fold: they shall make great noise by reason of the multitude of men.

The breaker is come up before them: they have broken up, and have passed through the gate, and are gone out by it: and their king shall pass before them, and the Lord on the head of them.
Micah 2:12–13

Introduction — Prophesying the captivity

If we had been with these excellent men of God — Micah, Jeremiah, and Isaiah — as they prophesied the captivity, then we could have seen that they were speaking with a lump in their throat. They were giving out excellent things — excellent, excellent, very good; 'There is a remnant left of us, a stump in the ground.' But if you listened to them, there was a sob in their voice; the tears were trickling down. (And God was at their back and putting their tears into his bottle, and writing them in his book.)

Another brother came along and said, 'Alas for the day! For the day of the Lord is at hand and as the destruction from the Almighty shall it come.' In the midst of it, the Lord whispered a word in the ear of Micah, and he said, 'Say this to my Jacob and this to my remnant of Israel — these godly women in the village and these men — this is to be a rod and a staff to them, for there is to be a dark valley ahead and it will last 70 years, and the holy city will be left for a long, long time.' Will he then forsake them for ever? O! No. 'I will surely assemble, O, Jacob, all of thee; I will surely gather the remnant of Israel; I will put them together as the sheep of Bozrah, as the flock in the midst of their fold.' And although the Lord's people suffered outwardly on account of the calamity that came upon the land as a whole — Daniel and Ezekiel and hundreds more — nevertheless they had the secret consolations of the Holy Ghost. The hand of the Lord was upon them for good, and the angel of the Lord encamped round about them. These prophecies were given to show them that the Lord would bring down his hand on Jerusalem, but would 'stay his rough wind in the day of the east wind'. He would never make a full end of them, because he had a cause, and the Redeemer was to come in the fullness of time, and hundreds of prophecies were to be fulfilled.

Captivity

The first thing to point out is that we are all in captivity spiritually just as these were literally. All who form the true Jacob of God are brought to know that they are in captivity. It is brought home to them by the Holy Spirit. Ask yourself — Did I find out that I was in captivity?

Captivity to sin

The captivity of my soul by nature is the captivity to the love of sin, and that means darkness, and that means rebellion, pride, and worldlimindedness and no appetite for the worship of God. Ask the Lord to show you that, and how you are a captive to prejudice and ignorance. I am a lump of ignorance, and although godly parents would tell us of the love of a divine Saviour, the whole thing would be 'as a root out of a dry ground' to us, unless the Lord in infinite pity anoint us with spiritual discernment. He may have to shake us over the mouth of perdition, so that we see the lake that burns with fire and brimstone, and see the waves splashing on the shores of eternity before we will be convinced.

Unless you have grace, you will be found cursing God in a damned eternity. Think of it. Remember that part of the work of those who will be sent away is to be cursing God. Ask the Lord — cry to him if you cannot pray — 'For the Redeemer's sake show me in mercy myself. What does that man mean, saying that my soul is a captive to pride, self-seeking and worldliness? Have mercy on my soul — *Thy mercy unto me do thou extend.'*

Seek in earnestness and seriousness down in your heart — plead with the Lord not to leave you shallow and superficial, with some nice morality on the surface, but without the truth of the law and the sanctifying truth of the gospel in you. Ask him to put it down into you and under you and wrapped round you so that the devil can never untie it. If your soul is bound up in the bundle of life and well knotted in the covenant, and you get Christ in the promise, then you are delivered from your captivity.

Who here has an appetite for the vicarious atonement of the Saviour? Show me a person who is getting a sweet taste of it, and if the vicarious atonement is as warm blankets round their soul, I would like to shake hands with them — and, with the blood of the covenant sprinkled on us, I think we will meet in heaven, even with all our failings.

Captivity to Satan
The next thing is, you are a captive to Satan. He can lead you captive at his will, and perhaps you will not know it is him. Perhaps you will be praying, and thinking that you have first class liberty, and all the time you are doing the work of the Devil. You were in captivity to sin and Satan; and usually where that is the case, you can speak about a hundred things — music, literature, moral philosophy, and what not. You can be a scholar, and be moral (and outward morality is a great blessing through restraining grace) but when a godly man or woman will speak to you about regeneration and about justification, your mouth is closed; or else you will put the cart before the horse and pretend you are godly and show yourself a fool, and show that you do not know what you are speaking about.

Captivity to God's law

We are not only captives to sin and Satan — what more? We
are captives to the law. Captivity to the law invariably
follows captivity to sin. Where there is the root principle
of hatred to holiness and opposition to God, which is in us
by nature — that man is in captivity to the law. That is
another way of saying that the law has something to do
with you; and however easy we may feel, and however far
away we are putting the day of death, if we go to eternity
without getting married to the Lamb and being united to
him, drinking in the merit of the atonement, and glorying
in the cross of the Lord Jesus Christ — if we have not that
in our consciences and hearts, the law sooner or later will
want to speak to you. 'O, but I have plenty of liberty in
the world. I pay my way at the butcher and grocer, and
what noise is being made about this holiness and my unholiness and sin and lack of preparation for eternity and
want of fear of God, and holy love and so on? I am free —
I am my own master. I am not going to pay attention to
you.'

'Stand here,' the Judge will say; 'do you love that law?'
Your conscience may be asleep and doped, but when the
Most High touches it it will burst like a volcano, and burst
on you, and you will agree with it when it charges you;
and although you may be able to hush it till death, I desire
to tell you in compassion and in love, you will turn against
yourself and waken in remorse — not repentance — it is
entirely different.

Unless you are in Christ Jesus and under the shelter of
his wings, there is nothing for you but the holiness of God
coming into conscious contact with your stark naked soul;
and if the infinite essence of the Most High comes judicially
into contact with your naked soul, you are bathed in hell.
That is what happens, and you are in a fixed state — you can
neither go north, south, east nor west — you are in the
presence of the being of the Most High there, and away
from his judicial presence you cannot get.

When your minister here, Mr MacKenzie, will be preaching to you,* watch with lynx eyes what he sets before

This sermon was preached in St. Jude's Church, Glasgow, in 1936.

you, and keep your mouth well open and swallow down the truth as it is in Jesus. For when the law turns on you, if you are not in Christ and in the cleft of the rock of ages, your condition will be truly awful. It cannot be put in language the anguish and remorse and pale face you will have that day, and you will go down before the look of the Most High under the sentence of the law.

We have to consider the two sides of the law — the demand of the law, and the penalty of the law. So long as we do not satisfy the demand of the law, we must face the penalty of the law. The Saviour met the demand of the law and he said, 'I love you and I will fulfil you.' And he met the penalty; 'I am to satisfy you. The sword of justice will pass into me, but it will not pass through me. I will open my bosom to the flaming sword. But not one inch will come out on the other side, for I am going to quench you in my soul and exhaust you for ever and ever.'

Deliverance

The next thing is the breaker, and we shall emphasise here that the Most High is the breaker. For he may use Ezra and others as ambassadors under him but in the person of the Saviour, the Lord Jesus Christ, the Bishop of our souls, he is the breaker — the divine breaker.

In eternity the Father said to the Redeemer, 'My dearly beloved Son, thou wilt be the breaker for them'. What did that mean? Christ in his work of redemption was to free them from the grasp of the law. Do you not mean the grasp of Satan? Which is first — freedom from the grasp of the law, or freedom from the grasp of Satan? There are people here tonight who know what the answer is, and I will not give it to you just now. You will set to and will roll up your sleeves spiritually and find out which is first, by the Shorter Catechism and the Confession of Faith, by watching what the minister here says, and what the elders say. And if you cannot arrive at it, ask them point blank and pocket your pride, and throw it in at the back of the fire — though alas it will come out again, the thief that it is — but seek to find out for your own good whether the work

of the Saviour has pre-eminently to do first with the power
of sin or with the claims of the law.

We will leave it at that just now, but I am afraid we are
giving away our little problem. He not only met the claims
of the law on behalf of the Israel of God; but he also now,
in virtue of that, received the Holy Spirit not according to
measure. He said, 'I undertake to meet the claims of the
law;' and the Father said, 'I promise to anoint you with
the everlasting Spirit, and you will also ransom them from
the grip of Satan.' The law says, 'I am very well pleased.
Every one that runs to the cleft of the rock I am delighted
with. Be gone the whole lot of you and flee to the rock of
ages!'

Once the Lord Jesus Christ, by the Holy Spirit, brings
them to the fold (as they gathered at the river Ahava) from
that point onwards till they reach the promised land in
glory he is still the breaker, and goes before them to lead
them to green pastures, guiding them in the good way. The
moment that they come to the fold they have passed
through the gate of the enemy, and out of the land of
captivity. 'Goodbye to the land of captivity!' Whoever
we are, and however the Lord may deal with us, he will
never forsake us. 'Goodbye Babylon!' — From that day
they are in a state of reconciliation. It is unchangeable,
as the divine essence is unchangeable. From that point
onwards, from the state of regeneration and from the passing out of the gate, they have entered into covenant and
they are joined to the Lord; and there is a flow of love
and liberty — a flow and reflow of light and life between
their heart and the heart of the Saviour. You have there
the beginning of the new life — reconciliation and
regenerating grace, and you are in the fixed estate of justification and adoption, and you go on with the Saviour as
the breaker up all the way until he brings you to the
Father's house, where the King passes in before you.

Remember me

Luke 23:39—43

We have here the account of the conversion of the penitent thief. In v. 42 we have the prayer, 'Lord, remember me', and in v. 43 the Redeemer's reply, 'Verily (or *Amen* or *As I live*) today thou shalt be with me in paradise.'

The Lord of glory was being crucified, the holy in the room of the unholy, to bring sinners to God, and yet from the point of view of his foes, we have a fearful manifestation of Satan and his presence. Even the two malefactors joined the cruel mob in jeering and mocking 'If thou be Christ, save thyself and us'. The spirit of Satan was in these men, though they were on the verge of eternity. All they desired was freedom from bodily sufferings. They had no desire whatever for the promised inheritance.

Scribes, pharisees and chief priests vehemently accused him; and others came out and mocked hin. This was their hour and the power of darkness. It is a fearful mystery how Satan was allowed in a spiritual way to attack the Redeemer at this time. 'The prince of this world cometh and hath nothing in me.' He was holy, harmless, undefiled and separate from sinners; and yet this was part of the cup which he drank lovingly for sinners. The very devils of Satan were permitted to attack the Redeemer, the infinitely holy One. It is likely that this satanic atmosphere prevailed in the bulk of those dwelling in Jerusalem at this time, though many of them got repentance later on.

And yet, into this prevailing darkness and enmity came the Holy Spirit to deal with this man's soul. He could not

71

lift a little finger to save himself, but God the Holy Ghost in the electing love of the Father and in the redeeming love of the Son came into his soul and so dealt with him that we are told he prayed 'Lord, remember me when thou comest into thy kingdom'. He must have undergone a wonderful, an extraordinary experience in a very short time. Shortly before, we find him railing on the Redeemer, but it probably was brought home to him that he who prayed 'Father, forgive them for they know not what they do' was indeed the Son of God, and that instead of asking for twelve legions of angels, he had lovely, holy compassion for poor sinners. It was just made real to him that the Father was *his* Father, and he the Son. And he realised that he was King of the Jews. Of course this was shouted at him in mockery, but it was made real to the thief that Christ was the King. Through the power of the Holy Spirit this thief was so melted and enlightened that he rebuked the other, and took shame to himself.

What a change! He was inwardly renewed by the Holy Ghost with life that shall never end. Life came into his soul — he could not tell how, nor can I — but he was led to pour out this prayer of holy worship and adoration, 'Lord, remember me when thou comest into thy kingdom.'

Probably, during his life, he was not even attending the synagogue. So long as he got money, by violence or otherwise, what did he care? Now he says 'Lord', by which he confessed, 'I was a Moabite, a son of the bondwoman; but Lord, I see a glory in thee and am sure that thou art the Son of God, the King of Israel. Do thou remember me. Entreat me not to leave thee.' He had the spirit of the prayer of Ruth. He was confiding in the Redeemer, his Lord and his God.

He wished the Lord to remember him *when he came into his kingdom.* What did he mean by this? One wonders — what did the man hear as he went about Jerusalem? Who knows, perhaps he was at the edge of some crowd, picking pockets, and heard something. Perhaps he heard Christ telling about the King coming, and separating the sheep from the goats. Or perhaps he was at the back of the Redeemer when he was before Pilate, and Barabbas was released. Perhaps he heard him saying, 'My kingdom is not of this world, else would my servants fight.'

In any case, Christ's reply was, 'Verily I say unto thee, *today*'. This seems to imply, *no delay until the Great Day*. Today I am going to Paradise, and thou shalt be with me today. What holy light, peace and life and sealing with the Holy Spirit were his, in virtue of the Redeemer's coming to seek and to save that which was lost. The Holy Ghost came in, never to go out; for where this sealing is, there is love to holiness and to the image of Christ. He had a new taste for Christ, and rejoiced in the liberty of the children of God. The Holy Ghost dwelt in him as the earnest of the promised inheritance. What a mystery!

In his youth he may have been taught Psalm 32 — we cannot tell. In any case now he had the spirit of it:

> *O blessed is the man to whom*
> *is freely pardoned*
> *All the transgression he hath done,*
> *whose sin is covered.*

and also —

> *Surely when floods of waters great*
> *do swell up to the brim,*
> *They shall not overwhelm his soul,*
> *nor once come near to him.*

The floods were up nearly to his teeth, to his very lips, and he was on the very brink of being drowned in a damned eternity, but '*Thus far thou shalt come and no further.* For Christ's sake go back, because this man was found in the everlasting covenant.'

And now his feet were on the rock. He had a new song in his mouth, even praise to our God. He could also say, 'The sorrows of death compassed me, the pains of hell gat hold upon me; I found trouble and sorrow. Then called I upon the name of the Lord. O Lord, I beseech Thee, deliver my soul. Gracious is the Lord and righteous, yea our God is merciful.'

There was joy in the presence of the angels of God over this repenting sinner. In a sense you may say that he died before he died on the cross. You may say 'This is a little

bit non-plussing'. But he died on the cross in a certain way,
crucified with Christ. If you were to ask the dying thief
'What does it mean to be crucified with Christ? You are not
to believe in him until you explain this,' he would say 'Oh,
I don't know what you mean; but he is altogether lovely.
It is for his sake alone if I am not to be lost, and he put
something in me, and he promised that I would be with
him before the sun went down.'

One should not be strong on these things; but I often
thought that, when he got that promise from Christ, he
would not feel any more the sufferings of his body. They
could break his legs if they liked, to hurry on his death;
but this promise was just like wine to him so that 'whether
in the body, or out of the body he could not tell'.

Before God

Now therefore are we all here present before God,
to hear all things that are commanded thee of God.
Acts 10:33

The Holy Spirit refers to those gathered in this place with
Cornelius, his kinsmen and near friends and Peter. They were
there before God. They knew that in a spiritual way they
were gathered in the presence of the Most High, the all-
knowing one, who sees the hearts of all.

While this expression 'before God' refers specially to
those gathered in Caesarea, we can apply it to Peter himself. While he was in Joppa he fell into a trance, but even
then he was before God, who had certain things to say
to him. He so guided him that, despite prejudices, he lived
and acted before God and set God before him in all his
ways. He thought on the vision which was three times given
to him, and the Holy Spirit sealed it on his spirit with the
words, 'Behold three men seek thee. Arise, therefore, and
get thee down and go with them, nothing doubting, for
I have sent them.' Peter was there before God.

Now we find Peter about to address those gathered with
Cornelius, having a peculiar sense of the Lord's presence.
(Surely God was fulfilling his promise, 'I will bring the blind
by a way that they knew not, I will lead them in paths
that they have not known'.) And Peter preached to them
Christ, the eternal Person of Christ and his finished work —
that he is Lord of all, including the Gentiles. This was the
copestone of the teaching of Peter's vision.

Peter preached before God. It is as if he were on oath
to declare the whole truth for which he would have to

give an account. By abounding grace he was speaking on
behalf of the Most High, and guided by him. He was holily
delighting in the Lord Jesus Christ, and in the Father for
giving the Son of his bosom, to abolish death and bring
life and immortality to light through the gospel. He had
seed for the sower and bread for the eater. Have you good
seed, Peter? Are you sure it is not bad, vain-glorious seed
you have — desiring to get a name as an orator, to please
itching ears, to please the flatterer? Or are you really seeking
to please God?

There is much vain-glory in the poor fallen, carnal mind;
and no doubt Peter would find it coming round the corner
again and again. But on this occasion he was given a great
deal of gospel liberty. There was seed for the sower; he had
plenty good, holy seed. And the Lord had secretly prepared
the ground, making those gathered at Caesarea meek and
lowly to receive the ingrafted word. In love to God, and at
the same time feeling how little he loved the Lord, Peter
by grace oozing out, was enabled to give bread to the eater,
and he got a good meal himself:—

> *They with the fatness of thy house*
> *shall be well satisfied.*

They were before God, before the high and holy one of
whom we are so ignorant, dear soul. The Lord provided a
table in the presence of the carnal mind. 'Lie down just
now, carnal mind. You've had a stroke, and hide in a corner'.
They were feeding on the Redeemer, and he became their
all in all. Their minds were satisfied, conscience and heart
were hanging on Christ while they fed on the manna in the
golden pot. They were lowlily receiving of the fulness that is
in Christ. They were appropriating the all-ness of Christ for
the all-ness of the soul of each; feeding upon him as their
passover Lamb, without blemish and without spot and
drinking in the meaning of his atoning death.

Rahab

Joshua chapter 2

Rahab belonged to the land which the Lord promised to give to the children of Israel for a possession and earthly inheritance. She was a heathen, and like others who were or will be brought from darkness to gospel light, and from being outlaws of heaven to have peace with God, she was by nature without hope and without God in the world. Not that Jericho and her people round about were without religious rites and practices. Far from it. They were idolaters, although the true God 'be not far from every one of us: for in him we live and move, and have our being.'

Along with idolatry there was another form of evil prevalent in this town and in the land generally; that is, immorality in various forms. Rahab was a harlot and seems, when the spies came, to have had a lodging-house or hostel for merchants and travellers in their goings and comings. The atmosphere was a heathen one, and to be a harlot and to have such a hostel would be at no great remove from one another.

It may be that the fact of her having flax on the flat roof is an indication of her being honourably employed at last, though her former designation stuck to her. At any rate the Lord prepared her, in a way she knew not, for the great change which followed. 'I will bring the blind by a way that they knew not, I will lead them in paths that they have not known. I will make darkness light before them, and crooked things straight. These things will I do unto them, and not forsake them.' (Isaiah 42:16)

How did Rahab come to know of Jehovah before the spies came? Answer — The news of God's doings at the Red

Sea soon spread. Pharaoh's name was a byword for power, dominion, and worldly glory. But God, who brought the Hebrews out of Egypt, was stronger than Pharaoh — even in heathen eyes. Neither the god of the Nile, nor of the valleys, nor of any hills, could resist Jehovah. Enemies faded before him as grass on housetops which withers before it is fully grown. We see that what Moses and Israel sang was fully and repeatedly corroborated afterwards. In Exodus Chapter 15 we have the whole song. 'I will sing unto the Lord, for he hath triumphed gloriously . . . he is my God, and I will prepare him an habitation, my father's God and I will exalt him . . . The people shall hear and be afraid . . . sorrow shall take hold on the inhabitants of Palestina . . . all the inhabitants of Canaan shall melt away ... By the greatness of thine arm they shall be as still as a stone, till the people pass over, O Lord, till the people pass over which thou hast purchased.'

So Rahab heard of God's deeds. She became convinced of God's will to favour Israel, of his power to cast down enemies, and to do for his people all that he promised. By the time that the spies came, her bent of mind and desire seems already much inclined towards the new disposition and character which the Israel of God manifests. She was now to be blessed according to the promise, 'I will bless them that bless thee' (Genesis 12:3).

The hand of God in his grace and providence is very evident in the guidance of the two spies to her house on that memorable occasion. It was reported that men of the children of Israel had come in, and the king sent officers to her to apprehend them. She determined to protect them, and mislead the officers. It was a time of trial, though God was with her to an extent she did not know. The action and decision were hers. The door of the tomb was now open. Was she to go out of this tomb by faith, and manifest the reality of it by receiving the spies with peace? Or, having heard of God and expressed herself as she did, was she now to draw back to perdition? Was Jericho to become a sepulchre for her as well as 'for them who believed not?' Was her home to become a family vault for her father and people — the door of it about to close down heavily for ever with her and hers on the inside, body and soul? She had taken the decision, hid the spies at grave risk to herself; and even in the midst of much ignorance, still she performed works as evidences of her faith when 'she had received the messengers, and had sent them out another way' (James 2:25).

In the event it became clear that she had not staked her all in vain on the covenant with its pledge and oath in the name of Jehovah (verse 12). The true token was there until the day of deliverance. She was preserved and openly acknowledged in that day.

Paul at Philippi

Acts chapter 16

There would have been many Jews in Philippi, and they would have been used to reading Moses and the Psalms, and the Prophets; but the world of Macedonia, and down the way of Achaia, and Greece generally on to Italy, was pagan and given to idolatry. Concerning those of Thessalonica, emphasis is laid on how God the Holy Spirit turned them from idols to serve the living God.

This was what they were needing in Macedonia. They were in a state of ungodliness; aliens and enemies in their minds, without hope and without God in the world. But the time to favour them had come.

In the early part of the chapter we have an account of the vision which the triune God gave to Paul. The vision was from the Father and from the Redeemer as the alone adorable head of his body the church. It was a revelation — a vision from the Most High through his Holy Spirit, for the glory of God and the good of the church. In this vision the Redeemer, by the Holy Spirit, brought this before the apostle, that there appeared a man of Macedonia. He likely showed him clothed with the clothing common in that place, whatever kind of garments they were in the habit of wearing. He heard this man say, 'Come over and help us'. He did not say, 'Help us with money; we are very poor, try to bring us some money.' Neither did he say, 'Help us, as Joseph helped the sons of Jacob in Egypt, with corn.' Evidently the sum and substance of the message put in this way to Paul in that dream was, to help them by bringing the gospel to the pagan world of Macedonia.

When Paul got this vision a promise, or promises, were implied in it. 'No weapon that is formed against thee shall prosper, and every tongue that riseth against thee in judgement thou shalt condemn.' In all their ways they would seek to acknowledge him, and he would direct their paths. So the one who commanded the wind and waves on the Lake of Galilee led them to Troas, and on to Philippi.

Here we come to read of Lydia, who heard at the riverside where prayer was wont to be made. (Very likely they were not permitted by the Roman officers to meet in the town itself; it was a Roman Colony.) Lydia — whose heart the Lord opened, that she attended to the things spoken. Though Paul planted and Apollos may have watered, along with Luke and Timothy, it was the Lord who opened her understanding and her heart.

Now may our prayer be, 'Open mine eyes that I may see my need of the Redeemer'. As the minister taught the little girl to pray, 'Show me myself,' and 'Show me thyself'. She saw the malady and on the other hand she saw the balm of Gilead, the holy remedy, and was brought to close in with the Redeemer on his own terms.

At the riverside, when Lydia was convinced and converted and bound up in the bundle of life with the Lord, Paul preached through the Holy Ghost. We may put it, Paul preached for eternity. The truth must have been very solemn — the holy word, which is the divine truth from the Father within the Godhead. So Paul spoke, and preached for eternity and in love, and yet all the time he looked to the Lord to break up the fallow ground.

Lydia was an honourable, hardworking woman. You would call her beyond reproach in the way of ordinary morality. But, from the spiritual point of view, the veil was still on her soul. And God, in the preaching of Paul, took off the veil; then she saw herself in the mirror of the law, and said, 'I am a woman of unclean lips, and I dwell in the midst of a people of unclean lips. What a thorn I am, and what a briar, and how fruitless I am. I have no holy fear, no consecration, and no holy insight!' She had need of being born of water and the Spirit as Jesus said to Nicodemus.

She was blessed, and she got in suitable measure what

Paul himself had, which is eternal life. She could say to herself, 'I have gone down to the grave in and with Christ, and
the life I now live in the flesh I live by dependence on the
Son of God.' Paul could say, 'He loved me and gave himself
for me.' And if you are crucified nevertheless living, the
Father gave you to him before the foundation of the world.
Your names are in the Lamb's Book of Life. The Son loved
you and died for you, as well as for Paul and for Lydia.

They had much trouble in the holy providence of the
Lord. When they got the vision, it implied that the Lord
would be with them and be as a wall of fire round about
them. But here they were attacked and smitten, then they
were reviled and persecuted and they landed in prison, and
the jailor was charged to keep Paul and Silas safely. Their
feet were made fast in the stocks; it did not look as if the
gospel was going to prosper in Macedonia.

One wonders how, in their bodily suffering, they could
pray and sing praises unto God. The Lord revived them in
spirit. He visited them with a time of holy refreshing from
the presence of the Lord. They got what we may call a
breeze of the Holy Ghost, of his grace to refresh them —
a gale of the holy love of God, Father, Son and Holy Ghost.
Perhaps they practically forgot their bodily weakness and
discomfort, and how their feet were fast in the stocks. The
Lord could do that.

They began to pray and sing praises unto God. We are
not told what praises they sang. No doubt they would
sing the Psalms; they were well at home in the Psalms.
Even in the days of their spiritual ignorance they would
be at home in chanting the Psalms in the synagogue.

Paul quotes one of them in the Epistle to the Romans,
Chapter 8, 'We are killed all the day long'. That is from
Psalm 44. They were only regarded as sheep for the slaughter.
A sheep in good condition would be more valuable to the
authorities in Philippi than two Jews causing a lot of trouble.

They may have been singing Psalm 9 — a Psalm peculiarly
appropriate.

> *God also will a refuge be*
> *for those that are oppress'd;*
> *A refuge will he be in times*
> *of trouble to distress'd.*

Another one might be Psalm 18:

> *And he upon a cherub rode,*
> *   and thereon he did fly;*
> *Yea, on the swift wings of the wind*
> *   his flight was from on high.*

The first reference here may be to the passage through the Red Sea, to the strong wind which came to fulfil his will. It was the same omnipotence, the finger of the Most High, which Paul and Silas were needing now at Philippi.

> *And from above the Lord sent down,*
> *   and took me from below;*
> *From many waters he me drew,*
> *   which would me overflow.*

Paul and Silas were not in waters literally; but they were in great difficulties, very great difficulties.

Then the Lord said to an earthquake, 'Work, earthquake'. By his own hand he touched the manacles of the prisoners. Everyone's bands were loosed. Can you tell how? Not for a moment. It was the invisible finger of the Most High. It was the Father. The sparrow falling on the ground, fowls of the air, fish of the sea, earthquakes and so on; all are under his control.

You may say, Paul's feet were not very fast in the stocks after all! For while they were singing there was an earthquake, and a man came running with a sword, going to kill himself. While he had a high enough countenance before, he came tumbling down. He fell flat before Paul and Silas, saying, 'What must I do to be saved?' He had a lot to be saved from.

He brings in the word 'do'; if I *do* something. A woman was saying to a doctor in Inverness that if only she felt she had something to do, she would feel easier. 'My dear woman,' said the doctor, 'Faith is not doing anything but resting on the work that Christ has already done.' That was a word in season to the woman; not *do, do, do,* but giving a bill of divorcement to our doing.

Now if Christ is precious to you, he loved you. You may

say to yourself, 'I can scarcely believe that'. 'If I could do something myself,' you might say, 'he ought to love me.' Stop that! May the Lord give us grace, that we be enabled to

> *Stand upon his merits,*
>   *and know no other stand,*
> *not even where glory dwelleth*
>   *in Emmanuel's land.*

What happened then? Paul began to preach, and the Holy Spirit melted the man and his household. They became like Lydia. They listened solemnly with lowliness. Grace came in, they did not know how. Grace melted them.

Grace is a great warrior. As was said of some man who was very reckless and foolish for drink, and he was fond of fighting men at markets; the Lord visited him and brought him round, over and down, to stand where the publican stood. When a certain elder was told that the man was converted he said, 'What a warrior grace must be that grace overcame that man!'

Now what was the sum and substance of the gospel which Paul preached; the God-given gospel, not sealed with the blood of bulls and of goats, but with the sacrifice of Emmanuel? Well, as to its holy object it was the glory of God; and as to the substance of it, it was *Jesus shall save his people from their sins.*

Zacchaeus

*And when Jesus came to the place, he looked up,
and saw him, and said to him, Zacchaeus, make
haste and come down; for today I must abide at
thy house.*

Luke 19:5

To whatever extent Zacchaeus grasped his lostness, and
whatever sense he had of it, we know that he had it in the
degree which the Lord saw needful. William Guthrie is of the
opinion that his sense of guilt was swallowed up in a few
moments in the holy liberty of the gospel. Whether in the
sycamore tree or in his house, in any case he came to know
that, though he should gain the whole world, it would not
profit him if he lost his soul. Who of us can grasp the
solemnity of the question, 'What shall a man give in exchange for his soul?' May the Lord give us the publican's
prayer — a secret cleaving to the Lord for eternity.

Zacchaeus was given a sense of need. It may have been
when the Redeemer looked up, and said, 'Zacchaeus', for
he called him 'Lord' (v. 8), and worshipped Him. He was
brought to know that Jesus knew his thoughts and spirit
and life. There is not much told of the work of the Holy
Spirit in melting Zacchaeus and convincing him of guilt,
yet in the needed measure the Redeemer, through the
Holy Ghost, brought this home to him. The whole have
no need of a physician, but those that are sick. We absolutely need him as the divine Saviour, or we perish for
ever.

There probably was an element of curiosity in Zacchaeus'
climbing the tree, but we believe there was far more than

this. He would have heard again and again of how the Redeemer preached to the poor and needy, to publicans and harlots. It is likely that he heard of the parables which we have in Luke 15 — the lost sheep, the lost coin, and the lost son, and that there is joy in the presence of the angels of God over one sinner that repents. Perhaps he also heard about the prayers of the publican and of the pharisee.

Here we have him in the sycamore tree. Probably no one saw him climb up, or was much interested in what the Redeemer would say or do to him. Perhaps he was so covered by leaves that there was very little of him to be seen, but he had a gnawing crave, secretly begotten in him by the Holy Ghost — a heart ache and an ache in his soul to get something from Christ, even while he was speaking to others.

The wonder is that, when addressed by Christ, Zacchaeus could come down at all. Afterwards he might say to himself, 'I was sure that no one saw me. I wonder that I was not paralysed with shock.' It is likely that he would have felt astounded were it not that his eyes and understanding were opened to see the Godhead of the Redeemer, the one who said 'Zacchaeus' to him. He could not say, 'Well, I saw him ask Peter or John who I was,' nor did he hear Christ say to any one, 'Did you see a man in a tree?' No, he said, 'Zacchaeus, make haste and come down,' and the word of a king was there. We may well conclude that there and then the divine new birth took place in the soul of Zacchaeus. He saw that here was one who knew him through and through. In calling him by name it was like saying, 'I am the Lord of Glory, entirely acquaint with all your ways'.

Zacchaeus came down and received him joyfully. He had the holy liberty of the gospel, his heart was opened with lowliness, wonder, simplicity; there was a divine resurrection in his soul, divine circumcision in his heart. He began to worship God in Christ, and to rejoice in Christ Jesus, giving a bill of divorcement to the flesh. He not only heard himself called by name with the ears of his body, but got spiritual power and life to close in with Emmanuel. He received Him joyfully. He got the light of the knowledge of the glory of God in the face of Jesus Christ.

'Unto you it is given in the behalf of Christ, not only to believe on him, but also to suffer for his sake.' He believed in his name and soon began to suffer. They told Christ that this was a notorious sinner, and it was not wise to keep company with him, but Zacchaeus was anointed with the Holy Ghost. If there was any psalm in the Book of Psalms in which he could rejoice, it is the 139th:—

> *O Lord, thou hast me searched and known.*
> *Thou know'st my sitting down,*
> *And rising up; yea all my thoughts*
>   *afar to thee are known.*

(If we have not Christ, this psalm will be just hell-fire to us; the eye of God on the soul, but never reconciled.) He would thank the Lord when he read in the psalm that even in his mother's womb his members all were writ. 'When he said to me, "Zacchaeus", something stole over me, came into my soul, and Christ was my water and milk.' The Holy Ghost came on the dry ground, and the promise began to be fulfilled, 'They shall spring up as among the grass as willows by the water courses'.

Christ went in to sup with Zacchaeus, and Zacchaeus with him. And the heart of Zacchaeus said 'Thou art the Son of God. Thou art the King of Israel;' and like Peter, he said 'Thou art the Christ, the Son of the Living God. Something has come into me. Thou knowest that though I have been a publican, cheating men and women, yet I desire to worship thee. Thou knowest all things; thou knowest that I love thee.'

Washing the disciples' feet

Jesus saith unto him, He that is washed needeth not save to wash his feet, but is clean every whit: and ye are clean, but not all . . . If I then, your Lord and Master, have washed your feet; ye also ought to wash one another's feet.
John 13:10,14

We find that the Saviour here put his 'Amen' to the fact that he was Jehovah manifest in the flesh. 'Ye call me Master and Lord, and ye say well, for so I am' (v. 13). He who could say, 'Before Abraham was I am' rose from supper, laid aside his garments and began to wash his disciples' feet. He who is the high and Holy One, who inhabits eternity, the infinitely holy one, the heart-knowing, heart-searching, heart-purifying one, is giving himself to poor, needy, rebellious sinners. May He be precious to us. The one who took a basin with water was in the Father's bosom before the mountains were brought forth. This is a revelation, the food of faith, and when this supernatural revelation enters into the soul, it is an earnest of heaven. May the Holy Spirit seal it upon us that he who said to Moses, 'I am that I am' was here in the upper chamber with his disciples and put his 'Amen' to the declaration that he was God.

The disciples were being taught gradually. There was a little leaven in their souls — Christ the hope of glory was there — and he would abide with them until the whole was leavened. The Lord's people are not perfect in this world. Like Peter they may sin sadly, but Christ never loses any of his sheep. He may have to give them many a stroke, but he searches them out in the dark day, and they will never perish. He will chastise them for their faults, but will fulfil his covenant promise to the Father and to them, that he will deliver them in six troubles, yea in seven there shall no evil touch them, till at last he presents them faultless before the presence of his Father with exceeding joy.

The New Testament Moses and Aaron

'If I then, your Lord and Master' — that is, in a spiritual way. The one who spoke was the New Covenant Moses, the divine prophet who cannot lie. It is he who speaks to you and to me here — the divine prophet set up from everlasting through God the Holy Spirit given to him not according to measure. (It was the Spirit who wrote the whole Bible, the spiritual library of the church of God in all ages, although in doing so he used agents, divinely directed men. If you love the Holy Spirit today, surely you love the Redeemer, and this chapter of God's word. If the substance of it is lovingly hid in your heart you desire to hearken to him and to be a servant of the New Covenant Moses.)

Then, Christ was also the divine Aaron, the substance of what he typically set forth. The Redeemer in his own way is the golden plate that was on the fore front of Aaron's mitre — *Holiness to the Lord* — to bear the iniquities of the children of Israel. If you know that truth, before you know where you are, it will wash the feet of your soul. The Redeemer is also the breast-plate, and the censer and the incense. If you love the Redeemer as your incense, then he has a basin of water and is cleansing your feet today. If you love the Redeemer because he brought everlasting satisfaction to the Father, and if this is sweet to you, then that satisfaction is brought into your soul. You say, 'That cannot be, because this satisfaction is infinite, and I am finite, and the infinite can never be contained by the finite'. That's good! I am pleased that you are well exercised. But the food of the Lord's people for eternity is the infinite satisfaction brought to the Father by Christ, and they feed on him whose atoning sacrifice has infinite efficacy; and if you spiritually receive this and like it, you are bathing your conscience in the atonement of Christ — whatever sin you may have committed, and in spite of the bad nature that is within. Where Christ as the New Testament Aaron is the incense and the sacrifice, the everlasting atonement is of such boundless, bottomless value that it can save even to the uttermost. None in the church below, nor any of the godly who have gone Home, can measure the uttermost in Christ. You may say, 'If you only knew what sins I committed — drunkenness, thieving, telling lies.' Go to your knees and tell the Lord about them, as if he did not know. Though you were a Manasseh, or all the vagabonds rolled together in one, over against the infinite merit of Christ's sacrifice it is as a grain of salt is in the salt cellar. If you are going to the Father's house, that is all you have, that is all your hope — the merit of Christ's atonement. You will be in hell if you are not in Christ Jesus and have a suitable, sweet, intelligent espousal to this atoning death of Christ.

He *can* save to the uttermost. He is the promise-making and the promise-sealing one. He is the New Covenant Moses and the New Covenant Aaron, and is incense in glory, the uncreated Angel with much incense. He has bells and pomegranates, and those in glory are hearing the bells, and extolling him for ever and ever. 'Worthy is the Lamb.' They hear the bells on the robe of their High Priest, who is sitting down at the right hand of the Father. How can the bells be heard when he is sitting down? Never mind! They are there, and he himself is every bell and pomegranate from Genesis to Revelation. There are those in this house today who hear what God the Lord speaks. The Saviour and divine Melchisedec is on the right hand of terrible majesty on high. Remember that without Christ we can never go to heaven, for God is an infinite consuming fire so that the seraphim veil their faces before the infinite majesty of the Most High, dear, dear soul!

The Saviour was pleased as part of the everlasting covenant to give this example of washing his disciples' feet. Simon Peter said, 'Thou shalt never wash my feet', or, 'It does not become thee to wash my feet'. But when Christ replied, 'If I wash thee not thou hast no part in me' Peter went the other way; the pendulum swung to the other extreme. 'My hands are not very clean, and my head — oh, the roving thoughts and the imaginations of my head! The thoughts of my head and heart are terrible, like midges that cannot be numbered.' 'Yes, but,' the Redeemer said, 'He that is washed needeth not save to wash his feet but is clean every whit; and ye are clean, but not all.' Christ knew that Judas would betray him. His was a terrible case, left to himself, and to the spirit of covetousness. We should ask the Lord to save us from what is in us — our carnal wisdom, and self will. Is it troubling yourself? Is it to you a body of sin and death? Do you desire to be saved from a self-pleasing spirit? May God the Holy Spirit make it a secret burden!

He that is washed

Here we have two things brought before us; 1. The washing of regeneration, and 2. The washing of the feet from time to time in sanctification.

1. Peter was washed in an absolute sense in regeneration. Peter was not perfectly holy, for Christ warned him, 'The cock shall not crow, till thou has denied me.' All the same Peter was perfect as regards the regenerating work of the Holy Spirit. All the true disciples were born again. They were brought to see that they were lost for eternity, that they were on the dunghill and the dunghill was inside them, but 'He raiseth up the poor out of the dust, and lifteth the needy out of the dunghill' (Ps. 113:7). In a suitable measure they knew their poverty. Have you had somewhat of that experience — to know yourselves as 'dunghill sinners?' Every one going in sincerity to the Lord's Table puts his 'Amen' to the truth that he or she is by nature on the dung-hill, and cannot think one holy thought. They are carnal, sold under sin, but they are secretly brought to discern the Lord in and through the gospel. All are brought with a load of guilt, and a load of unholiness — a double load — to see Christ, and to touch him with the supernatural touch of regenerating grace, to get a God-created inclination to say, 'That's the gospel'. These are the Lord's covenant people for all eternity. God will not be mocked, but he will not mock you if you are putting your 'Amen' to the gospel, if with cordiality you receive the gospel; for in the act of receiving the gospel, you receive Christ. If to your

heart the gospel is honey; if you see yourself as a lump of unholiness, but the gospel as holily excellent, then you will be pleased with Christ. Grace may yet be as a grain of mustard seed, but where he begins the good work he will carry it on. Owen says, 'Faith, in the first place, is a receiving of the revelation of the gospel, and this is a means of resting on Christ Himself.' When Peter received Christ he was washed with the washing of regeneration, and his prayer was, 'May thyself come into my soul and stay in.' Then something happened, that he pounced on the person and finished work of Emmanuel in the gospel. This is the act of a regenerated soul. 'Jehovah our Righteousness' becomes your very own. Faith is a disposition of soul to pounce on the Redeemer.

2. Though perfect in justifying righteousness, the soul still has need of its feet being cleansed. Peter was justified, dear man, yet once and again he fell into the mire (though not back under condemnation, for that cannot be). He said something once which made the Saviour answer, 'Get thee behind me, Satan'. Then, again, Satan was whispering to Peter, and making a fool of him: 'Though others might leave Christ, you will stand by him.' Peter did have genuine love to the Saviour; but Peter did not know 'Peter', and Peter was to climb down and climb down. This creeping down is a great part of the life of sanctification. It is a promising sign, to be climbing down. People naturally like to climb *up*. Now, now, Peter, there is a cock, and it is going to crow, and you will deny me. Unbelievable! But, oh, later we hear a maid say to Peter, 'Thou also wast with him'. Ah, when Peter was left to carnal wisdom the fear of being arrested, and perhaps crucified, took possession of him and he used strong language, and yet he had faith all the time. 'I have prayed for thee.' We cannot understand how the tide of grace can be at such a low ebb in the soul; and yet faith is there, even in this sad temptation. May you and I be preserved from thinking censoriously of Peter, as if we were up on some big stool and could afford to speak. All this was over-ruled for Peter's good. He was in the intercession of Christ. He went out and wept bitterly. It must have been an *awful* Sabbath day for Peter. The Lord preserved his reason, but what anguish he suffered because he did what he did and said what he said; for he

did love the Redeemer, and was united to him for eternity! When he rose from the dead, he met Peter alone. We are not told what happened then, but we may be sure that he kissed the soul of Peter. He took a basin and water, and washed the feet of Peter, and strengthened and refreshed him. 'Be not grieved nor angry. I am Joseph your brother.' Though he did not take a basin and water literally, he said to him in effect, 'I must wash your feet; there is a good deal of dust on your feet.'

How to wash one another's feet

Later, at the lake side there were six of the disciples in a boat, and the Saviour was on the shore, and a fire of coals and fish laid thereon and bread. The Saviour said, 'Bring of the fish which ye have now caught. Come along now Peter, and I'll wash your feet.' How? 'Lovest thou me?' At last Peter said, 'Thou knowest that I love thee.' 'Thou, the high and Holy One, knowest that I love thee.' The Lord never said a word to Peter doubting the sincerity of this; but gave him a command, 'Feed my sheep, feed my lambs.' This is a beautiful, God-glorifying example of taking a basin and water and washing the feet of Peter. It is as if Christ said to him, 'If you come across this man or that woman, you'll copy me, and wash their feet in a suitable way. Seeing you went through this yourself, you will know how to help and soothe and refresh by the blessing of the Lord, and so know how to wash one another's feet.'

Another example we have on the day of Pentecost, when three thousand were regenerated by the Holy Spirit. Peter was the mouth-piece and his ministry was blessed. He spoke of Psalm 16, 'Thou wilt show me the path of life.' We must conclude that while Peter was preaching by the love of the Holy Spirit, his feet were being washed anew. Peter must have felt his need of daily cleansing. But 'Oh! It washes my feet to be allowed to preach on Psalm 16, to tell how the Redeemer went to the grave, and took the sting out of death and went to glory.'

Moving on to 1 Peter, we find basins of water to wash the feet of multitudes till the blast of the 'last trump'. They will thank God that ever he gave a basin of water to Peter, even this one, 'Whom having not seen ye love, in whom though now ye see him not, yet believing ye rejoice with joy unspeakable and full of glory.' Do you believe in the gospel as the truth of God, spoken through Christ, and do you desire to be washed in the fountain opened for sin and for uncleanness? Where that is, by the unction of the Holy Spirit, you are a believer in the Redeemer, and need to be washed like Peter, all the day long.

In all the gospels there are plenty of basins of water. Seek to wash others, lovingly and quietly. Watch not to say anything to hurt people unnecessarily, but to be a helper to them, so that they would have to say, 'I like even to be corrected by that man and woman for they have a love to my soul, and desire my well-being. They seem to see more faults in themselves than ever they find in others.'

'If I then, your Lord and Master, have washed your feet, ye also ought to wash one another's feet.'

5.
Extended comments on Scripture passages

The Living way

I am the way, the truth, and the life
John 14:6

It is likely that, when Aaron went into the holy of holies, only a portion of the veil was lifted; but Christ's holy human nature was rent from the top to the bottom when he said 'It is finished', and committed his soul into the bosom of the Father. On the third day he rose from the grave, and later he ascended on high, and officially entered into the holiest, even into heaven itself, and stayed in. This is the new way in contrast with the old way.

Christ is also the Life, or the living Way. The old way, by the blood of bulls and of goats was a dead way. It was but a shadow of good things to come, 'For it is not possible that the blood of bulls and of goats should take away sins.' In the case of the Redeemer, his was a living sacrifice. Rev. John MacRae used to say, 'He passed through death alive'. He was still God, and had a hold of his human soul and his human body, even when they were separate. These have been compared to a sword and a sheath. When the Redeemer died, the sword of his soul was drawn out of the sheath of his body, but his Godhead had hold of both; and in the resurrection morning, the sword was put back into its sheath.

He is the living One in glory, with the worth of his death, promising himself to your conscience and to mine as freely offered in the gospel. He is alive in glory, and he gives life through the Holy Spirit to all the heirs of salvation. The great matter is to be of them. Do not say, 'If I feel better, I will apply to Christ for life, and for the new heart,' but may you be made secretly restless until you get a bed in Christ, till your conscience gets peace in Emmanuel.

The red heifer

Numbers 19

All the Old Testament types and shadows had their fulfil-
ment in Christ, whose death gave meaning to the Old Testament.

The heifer was to be without spot or blemish, and one
on which never came yoke. So was the great Antitype holy,
harmless, undefiled. From all eternity he lay in the bosom
of the Father — never had yoke come upon him. But he came
under the law, and was made a curse for us.

And what do we make of the cedar wood and hyssop
and scarlet? One commentator suggests that it is the pride
and meanness of man that is to be burnt up. But I do not
feel too easy about this, and prefer to think of these as
signifying the promises. And how can they be said to be cast
into the midst of the burning of the heifer? Well, when the
Redeemer was in Gethsemane and on the cross, every
promise — the whole word of God — was with him there.
Psalm 22 was with him there. The promises went into the
grave with him, and rose again with him. And now, 'The
blood of Jesus Christ the Son of God cleanses us from
all sin.'

'And for an unclean person they shall take of the ashes
of the burnt heifer of purification for sin, and running
water shall be put thereto in a vessel. And a clean person
shall take hyssop and dip it in the water, and sprinkle it . . .'
What, do you think, is the running water? The gracious,
sanctifying influences of the Holy Spirit. Are you praying
now that he sprinkle upon your soul the merits of the death
of Christ, the ashes of the heifer? May he come, wave upon
wave, that your peace be as a river, and your righteousness
(your cleansings, and therefore your righteousness) as the
waves of the sea.

If you are complaining of your sins, just take a good
grip on a handful of the ashes of the red heifer. Sprinkle
them on yourself, and ask the Lord to mix it with faith in
your heart. On the third day the man who was ceremonially
unclean put on the ashes — which represented the merit
of the death of Christ. You put these ashes on your own

heart, and on the seventh day you will be without blame before him in love.

A Lively hope

He hath begotten us again unto a lively hope by the resurrection of Jesus Christ from the dead.
1 Peter 1:3

Is there such a thing as a dead hope; and if so, what is the difference between a dead, or a deadly hope, and a lively, or living hope? There is a dead hope which will never bring a soul to heaven. One example of this is the assertion of the Jews, 'We have Abraham to our father;' to which the Saviour replied, 'Ye are of your father the devil.' They were cherishing a dead hope. This is sadly common in the visible church; cherishing a false hope, having a gospel which is not a gospel — thinking God to be the Father of all in the same way.

I was thinking in connection with a dead hope that it is like a piece of rusty barbed wire, which might be lying on the road, and if it comes in contact with the tyre of your car, it punctures it before you know where you are. It is something useless and injurious. But there are wires that are useful and in excellent condition, with electric current running along them — live wires. Where a true believer is, he has been begotten again. In the mercy of God that soul has a well grounded hope with gospel, holy reality in it. The only way to be a live wire is to have the spirit of the gospel. It is the same soul, and the same faculties, but the bias and disposition are changed. Holiness comes in, and God the Holy Spirit creates the soul anew in Jesus Christ, so that he is charged with the spirit of power and love and a sound mind.

The current is greater in some than in others; some have much more of the Spirit of Emmanuel than others. But all who are begotten again unto this lively hope are changed through the abundant mercy of God the Father in giving the Redeemer, and through the abundant mercy of the Redeemer who had the infinite worth of his death in the hollow of his hand when he rose from the dead, and when he took his precious blood into the holiest of all.

If that is precious to your soul tonight, then you are blessed. You will have groanings and mourning because of what you find within. But 'Blessed are they that mourn, for they shall be comforted'. The Lord has handkerchiefs to wipe the tears from the eyes of his people, boxes of lovely handkerchiefs in the promises of the gospel. He keeps their tears also in his bottle.

If you are seeking to be soaked in him, then you have the earnest of the inheritance — a new covenant hope. What are we but empty pails, full of holes, and the only way to fill such a vessel is to keep it steeped in water.

Lord, teach us, melt us, save us from ourselves; breathe on us and bless us with a current of the Holy Spirit, for Jesus sake. This is the beginning of the everlasting inheritance.

Isaiah 40

He sitteth on the circle of the earth, and the inhabitants thereof are as grasshoppers. (v. 22) These things teach us how frail we are. But the Redeemer who grasped our nature to conquer death and hell for all who flee to him (he will in no wise cast them out, but put his arms about them) he is eternal and infinite. There is an infinite glory pertaining to the one God, infinitely above the glory of the created angels. He is inconceivably glorious in wisdom and majesty, dear soul. We should ponder these things, for we must yet lie down and rise not, till the heavens be no more.

All the nations that ever were or are, are less than nothing, compared with him. The Lord bless us with prostration of

spirit to realise that he is infinitely glorious — even in Gethsemane, though he was as he was, and on Calvary. If it
had been the will of the Father that his glory should shine
forth, all about him would have been consumed — burnt
to a cinder.

The nations are nothing before him who is everywhere.
He is, judicially, in the place where there is no hope; and
that is a cause of horror to those in chains of darkness,
preserved to judgment until the great day.

'He counts the number of the stars; he names them every
one.' Perhaps Isaiah quoted Psalm 147 in verse 26 *He calls
them all by name by the greatness of his might; for that he
is strong in power; not one faileth.* Perhaps the metaphor is
that, it is like the General of an army; when inspecting his
troops, he calls out the names of the men, and they answer
that they are present. So the Lord keeps all the stars in
being. Not one says, 'May I fall out? I feel unwell, I need
treatment in the sick bay.'

We see here his self-existence. By him all things were
called into being, and by him all things consist. That is,
until the time when he rolls away the heavens like a thread-
bare garment. Look up, let me see, Chapter 51 in Isaiah,
and there you will find a feast of manna — food to eat that
the world knows not of. 'Lift up your eyes to the heavens
and look upon the earth beneath; for the heavens shall
vanish away like smoke' — like smoke coming out of a
chimney; you cannot get a grip of it. It was coming out
of that chimney there, and now where is it? It might be
over in Cromarty for all you know. 'But my salvation shall
be for ever, and my righteousness shall not be abolished.'
These are arm in arm — the righteousness of God and his
salvation — salvation from the subtlety of sin, the un-
knowableness of sin; and when he begins the good work,
he will carry it on to the day of Jesus Christ.

The Father commanded his Son to ride on an ass, and on
a colt, the foal of an ass. He did it, and then the time came
when a great company gathered, and they smote him on
the cheek, and said, 'Prophesy unto us, thou Christ. Who is
it that smote thee?' It was he that sat on the circle of the

earth they smote. And he could say to them, 'I have prophesied to you since the Garden of Eden, and, if you were not
so drunk, and so mad spiritually, you would know it.' He was
bringing in everlasting righteousness, bringing life for the
soul and immortality for the body to light through the
gospel. Ask yourself now, if these men did not get a drink
of the meaning of the atonement, where are they today?

Washing and renewing

*The washing of regeneration, and renewing of the
Holy Ghost.*
Titus 3 :5

However little you may grasp of what the washing of
regeneration and renewing of the Holy Ghost mean; yet,
if you love the truth and rejoice in it, you may go away
possessing it. If you love the way of salvation and are
enabled secretly to climb down and say, 'I am foolish,
disobedient, deceived. I have been going astray from the
womb, doing iniquity.' Yet there is something in you that
loves this way of salvation. Is it wine and milk to your
soul? Then, I would conclude that you are washed with
the washing of regeneration and the renewing of the Holy
Ghost. A person may have a blessing yet not be able to
tell much about it. This is the secret work of the Holy
Ghost in the soul.

You may say 'I would like to think that I confide in
Emmanuel, but I do not feel that the Holy Ghost is shed
on me abundantly'; but if you love Christ, it is because
the Holy Ghost *is* shed on you abundantly. If you have
only a drop of love to Christ, it puts you among the living
in Jerusalem; there must be an abundant shedding abroad
of the Holy Ghost to cause such a renewing. You may
fear you have not got it, yet if you have a longing to be
foursquare with the gospel and to live a life according to it,
then the Holy Ghost has come into you, dear soul.

This is the secret, internal, invisible, work of the Holy Spirit. We need not say that regeneration follows washing. It is the washing of regeneration, or of genesis over again — the beginning over again — a re-begetting within the soul. Like a flash of lightning you are washed and you take to the washing. A new thing has begun in the soul — life that shall never end. God the Holy Ghost creates this, and with it comes forgiveness of sins. 'I have blotted out as a thick cloud thy transgressions.'

Look now at the other side: 'And, (or *even*,) the renewing of the Holy Ghost.' Renewing means making fresh again. Instead of being as we are in Adam — a stinking corpse full of wounds and bruises and putrifying sores, full of malice and envy — here we have not only washing, but the wiping out of sin, renovating by the Holy Ghost to become holy, given an holy disposition, a taste for holiness. The washing of regeneration is like one side of the penny, and the renewing of the Holy Ghost is the other. You cannot have the one without the other, nor can you say that one is before the other.

A table for me

Thou preparest a table before me in the presence of mine enemies.
Psalm 23:5

There are many great enemies before whom this table is spread — the world, the flesh and the devil.

You who are mothers know what it is to set apart a special day of the week to bake for your families. You will roll up your sleeves, and work so heartily; and if the children are late in coming home from school you say 'Oh, they will be hungry tonight. I wonder what can be keeping them. I must prepare a good dinner for them tonight.'

Well, the Saviour prepared a great feast for his children. And what was the day on which he did so? It was on Calvary;

and never did a mother so lovingly or so willingly roll up her sleeves to bake for the needs of her children as did Christ set himself to prepare this feast for his church. In some houses I see cookery books — for example *Mrs. Beeton's Cookery Book*. What was the book which Christ had? It was the eternal covenant. And the Father said to his Son, 'You'll put this in it, and you'll put that in it.'

The school to which Christ's children have to go is the school of the law; and after they have been taught many lessons there they run home in a day of grace, with an appetite which they never felt before, to partake of the feast of the gospel.

People sometimes say, when passing up their cups, 'Just one third, please.' But Christ desires us to pass up our plates today; and he will give us, not one third, but three thirds full of everything to satisfy our mind, conscience, heart and will, that our experience be like David's, 'My cup runneth over.'

All the family requires food. Johnny may be fifteen, Willie thirteen, Mary seven, and Angus one and a half, but each must have food suited to his age. Even the babe of six months requires milk to sustain him. So are Christ's spiritual family. We have seen a great many sitting at his Table here today* — some ripe in years and experience, and a few young ones also. But each will be fed by himself, according as his age requires.

We have had lessons within the past year. Some whom we loved and who were in this House Beautiful with us have been taken to be with himself, and we do not know who may be next. Sometimes he is pleased to take the younger ones before the older. But oh! to be ready at his coming, when 'the marriage of the lamb is come, and his wife hath made herself ready.'

'Blessed are they which are called to the marriage supper of the lamb.'

*This address accompanied the serving of the Lord's Table.

An example of how Mr Macfarlane used his books. This is his copy of Halyburton's Works (see pages 26-29).

6.
Portraits of Scripture characters

Matthew

We do not read much about the sweet conversion of Matthew himself. The Redeemer called him, and he obeyed; he arose and followed him. Afterwards he made a feast. Perhaps he said to quite a few, 'Come and help me to make a supper,' and he asked his fellow sinners along to his house. Perhaps he said to them: 'Maybe the Master himself will speak a word, and you will get a blessing for eternity.' We do not know, but perhaps that was so, and all those in that company are with Matthew himself in glory. At any rate he did his best.

Abraham

What stair did you come in by, Abraham? Did you break a pane of glass and come through? No, I did not want to be a thief or a robber. How many steps were on the stair you came in by? There were four steps. Tell us them.

1. The first was, knowledge as to my guilt and misery and that I would be for ever miserable if I were not washed.

2. The second was, enlightenment in the knowledge of Christ. Did Abraham get that? Yes. 'Your father Abraham rejoiced to see my day, and he saw it, and was glad.' Abraham clapped his hands for joy. Are you sure? Yes. Was

Abraham ever at a dance? As surely as David danced before
the Ark of God, so surely did the conscience of Abraham
dance before the promised Christ.

3. The next thing is that, if you lie down on him — unworthy and feeling your unworthiness — notwithstanding,
lie down on him, and are enabled, with a willing will and a
warm heart to the Redeemer, to accept him, he is yours.

4. What is the next step? Well, what I say to women at a
marriage service is something like this. I say first to the man,
'Do you promise to be a loving and faithful husband?'
And he says, 'Yes;' and then I say to the woman, 'Do you
take this man to be your husband, and do you promise to
be a loving, faithful and obedient wife?' 'Yes.' The Spirit
said to Abraham, 'Christ is coming of your seed, and do
you promise by the grace of God, and on the ground of
what the Redeemer is to do, to take him as your righteousness, your foundation, and forerunner, and your all and in
all — your Head, your living and energising Head, and do
you promise to marry him spiritually, and be a living and
faithful member of his body?' And Abraham said, by renewing grace and faith from heaven, and getting drops from the
fullness that is there, *I will*. God said to Abraham, 'Here is
a promise for you Abraham; hang your soul on it.' And in
a day of mercy, through the Holy Ghost, the soul of
Abraham took a leap from nature to God. His heart was
one with God, and he would put his Amen to all that was
said against him:—

> 'You are a beggar, Abraham.'
> 'Amen, Amen.'

With this promise in hand, Abraham was a debtor and a
two-handed beggar.

Abraham got a good, loving grasp of God's covenant.
Abraham looked at it knowingly — the eyes of his understanding were opened to see it. He got a view through the
Spirit which set his conscience dancing, and he got a drink
of the blood. He knew the Lord as a just Lord and a Saviour.

Abraham had grace already — he was a spiritual eye-witness
of the glory of the Lord when he came out of Ur of the

Chaldees. Many a promise he got; he was promised a son, who would be given to him in God's good time. Both Abraham and Sarah needed to be taught to exercise patience. They derived many a lesson from this — how they had to wait on the Lord's time, and not trust in their own carnal wisdom, which only brings trouble with it. However, when the time came, Sarah exercised special faith and Isaac was conceived.

Abraham's faith was put to the proof at this time, and a very severe test it was. A burnt offering was to be burnt completely. The Lord met with him, and it was sealed on him that this offering up of Isaac was the will, the holy will of the Lord. The Lord pointed out the spot to him in some way or other; it is not for us to enquire as to how. It must have been in some ways a great burden on the heart of Abraham — What now of the promised seed? But every grace that was needful was being exercised at this time — holy love and obedience, worship and filial fear. He believed that he would receive Isaac again, even though he were offered up. He had such faith that he did not say, 'What is to happen to me? and what is the Canaanite of the land going to say when he hears that Isaac was offered up by his own father?' See the holy self-denial in Abraham.

Notice how, in verse one of Genesis chapter 22, God said, 'Abraham.' And he answered 'Here I am.' I do not ask you to agree with me if you do not desire to do so; but, as I see it, the moment that the Lord said, 'Abraham', he anew manifested his glory and Abraham said,

'Amen, here I am.' What is the meaning of this? Just this, that Abraham said 'I am out and out, body and soul, for thee. I got such a view of thy glory that it has blessedly blinded me.' (As a man when looking at the sun or other brilliant light inadvertently, when he turns his eye on other things, sees black shadows on them.)

'I got such a view of the glory of the Sun of Righteousness that I had to say, *Here I am! My heart is for thee. Body and soul, spirit and conduct, I am for thee.* Without any disrespect to Sarah or Isaac, I am blessedly blind to what Sarah will think or say, or to what Isaac will think or say. Come along Isaac!'

Abraham was in a fever of glory, boasting in the Redeemer. His heart was mounting up with wings as eagles. 'Here, Isaac, lie down here' — and Isaac had no more thought of refusing than if he were a babe a week old. There is every reason to believe that Isaac had gracious wisdom in him, and loved the will of God, taking the side of God against his own feelings. They were both worshipping the Lord when the offering was about to be killed.

Peter

Did you ever cut yourself with stones? Peter was a great and godly man, but before he knew where he was he was cutting himself with stones, and made himself very ragged, the dear man. But Christ healed him and raised him and made him a lowly, loving servant of the Most High.

Jacob

Before Esau sold his birthright, the line of the holy family would have been Abraham, Isaac, *Esau*. But when he sold his birthright, he was struck off, cut off out of the line, and Jacob took his place; these things were of course over-ruled by the Most High, for his own wise ends.

Jacob and his mother were involved in bearing false witness to Isaac. It looks as if his mother really influenced him, and Jacob was overborne, so that he lied to Isaac. But Jacob was chastised for it, and he bore the chastisement. That is a mark of God's people, that they get grace to kiss the rod of chastisement. See how he got Leah instead of Rachel. Whatever she said to him — whatever lies she told him or did not tell him — she said in effect to Jacob, 'I am Rachel, and you have loved me, and laboured seven years for me.' Perhaps they put a veil on her, and it was in the dark anyway. And again, Jacob was out in the frost and cold, and his wages were changed seven times. So he was chastised, and he got repentance.

It is very remarkable, just in passing, to notice about the heap of stones which was erected as a witness between Jacob and Laban. It was called *Mispah* and *Galeed* — the heap of witness. It was then, when they agreed that neither was to pass over that heap to the other for harm, that the host of God appeared to Jacob. He called it Mahanaim. For all our purposes we may call it a plural form, though it really means one plus something.

We do not know how many Jacob saw — if it was a thousand, or five thousand angels he saw. (Probably it was in a vision that he saw them.) At any rate he saw them in their thousands, passing before the great white throne. Whether it was before and behind they were, or on this side and that, at any rate there they were, rank after rank, like the 51st Division, and Jacob had a review day.

Then you remember how he lost Joseph, and so on till you come to the great prophesy, 'Until Shiloh come, and unto him shall the *crowning* of the people be.' On his head are many crowns; the crown of creation and of providence, the crown of grace and of glory. They would all come to seek to touch the hem of his garment, to get to kiss him, as commanded, so that he would not be angry with them.

Now it was not that Jacob was worthy that he was put in, instead of Esau. He said himself he was unworthy. He was just dust and ashes. So all the godly find themselves to be dust, dust. And they say, 'I am dirty dust at that — oh, what dirty dust I am!' But Christ himself becomes all things to them. He is their wisdom and righteousness. Not that they are as wise as he, for he is infinitely so; but they receive out of his fullness. And there are some looking at me tonight, too, and the Lord says, 'They shall be mine, in the day when I make up my jewels.'

We had better not gather stones to throw at poor Jacob's faults — as far as possible, it is wise and loving and tender to cover over the faults of the people of God. And if we have to mention them, as David had to be dealt with, and Peter had to be dealt with, and Jonah too — the Lord put him into the whale's belly to learn a lesson or two — let us do it in love and tenderness. It will not do for you and me to speak superciliously of Jacob — 'What right had you to be deceitful and so subtle?' We need not go past our own bosoms. 'The heart is deceitful above all things, and desperately wicked.' Even where the Lord begins the good work and carries it on; if left, we break out again almost as if we had no grace at all. We should see then our need of the Saviour and his finished work, on account of seeing the old Jacob in here, and that deceit and subtlety which poor Jacob exhibited. Jacob was very beautiful at last, and is today beautiful in the palace above.

Simeon

Simeon took hold of the child Jesus, and the child took hold of him. The babe was in Simeon's arms, and Simeon was in the arms of the babe.

The women at the tomb

For fear of the angel, the keepers became as dead men. If he were to exert his power, they and the whole world could instantly be in a cinder; but he turned to the women and said, 'Fear not ye; for I know that ye seek Jesus which was crucified. These keepers have fallen in a faint or something over there, but come you and see the place where the Lord lay. As he told you, he is risen, and because he lives you shall live also.' We believe that the brightness of the angel lit up the sepulchre, and enabled these godly women to behold the empty grave and the grave clothes and the napkin that was about his head. They saw and believed. 'Now,' said the angel, 'run and tell the disciples that he is risen from the dead.'

Away they went, and while they obeyed they met Melchizedek, their heavenly Melchizedek, bringing forth for them bread and wine. He himself was their bread and wine, and will be to all eternity.

Abel and Enoch

Abel had a revelation from the Most High through Adam that the seed of the woman should bruise the head of the serpent. He had sufficient in the first promise to teach him. In it Abel heard the Lord say, 'I promise to be your shepherd and attend to you, Abel.' He saw him who is invisible, and believed that the divine messenger of the Father was to be made of a woman. How do you know the Most High, Abel? — 'O, by his secret power he gave me a secret liking for him. There is something in self that I hate and to which I wish I could give a bill of divorcement for eternity. I see that he is just and yet a Saviour for the sake of the Lamb who is to come.' Thereby Abel had evidence of things not seen.

In himself, Abel was no better than Cain. But by implication Abel acknowledged that he got Christ in the promise, that he was lifted off self-sufficiency, stripped stark naked as he saw the glory of God in the law, and saw that he was ripening for a lost eternity. He put his *amen* to the glory of God in the law, and also to the mercy of Christ in the promise; and like a flash he was at peace with God through Christ Jesus.

He beheld the glory of God in the face of Jesus Christ, and that was the beginning of eternal love and worship.

Power came into his soul, although the old, terrible nature was still there. There was a softness of heart implanted, a secret principle with longings after Christ, to put him on, and get sweet tastes of the Redeemer, and of the covenant of grace.

It is very likely that Cain tried to put in a wedge between Abel and the promise, or the Saviour through the golden pipe of the promise. I do not state this as a dogma, just as an opinion, that Satan was permitted to use Cain as a tool, and yet Cain did it of his own free will.

While Cain sought to separate between Abel and his God, eternal love and life came into the heart of Abel, and he had the equivalent of 'I am persuaded that neither death nor life . . . nor any other creature . . . shall be able to separate us from the love of God which is in Christ Jesus our Lord.' Once eternal love and life came into his soul, Christ in the promise was sweet and his hope for eternity. He would rather die than part with him. (Cain is quite conscious today that he slew his brother, and will be to all eternity. The eye of God is eternally upon the lost, and they can never escape from it. It is very little we can grasp of this awful thought.)

Abel was married to his Saviour and to God the Father, however little he might know about the three persons of the Trinity. He knew what was suitable, and went away to his Father's house as to his soul, while his body rests in the grave until the resurrection.

Through the translation of Enoch the Most High was revealing to the church that every believer is so precious to him that sooner or later he will save all, body and soul. When Christ has for ever bruised the head of the serpent, he will present them faultless in the presence of his glory, with exceeding joy.

The two men on the road to Emmaus

There were once two men walking sadly away from Jerusalem. They were in the valley of the shadow of death, but it cannot be said that they feared no ill. They had many fears. Their step was so heavy that you would think they had lead in their sandals, and lead on their backs; and then, this same Jesus as followed his people through the wilderness joined himself to them and the manna came pouring down from heaven. Then they had the golden pot and their hearts rejoiced in such a way that whether in the body or out of the body they could not tell.

Noah

What kind of faith did Noah have? He had the same kind of faith as had Abel and Enoch. It was sealed on Noah for eternity that the Redeemer was to come. Like Abraham, he saw his day afar off, and was glad. He got holy quietness of soul, peace with God, and saw that the Lord could be righteous for the Redeemer's sake in saving him from the pleasant poison of sin, from a self-centered principle and from self seeking, and the guilt which this inevitably entails.

Noah was blessed as Enoch was, with the evidence of things unseen, especially concerning the redemption to be obtained by the Lord of Glory in the fullness of time. But also he had the evidence of things unseen in providence. As Enoch had concerning his translation so had Noah, even though his body should lie in the grave until the resurrection. 'And unto them that look for him shall he appear without sin unto salvation.' All those had the evidence of things unseen. The Saviour gave them understanding to receive the word from his mouth, to know the meaning of it, and to act accordingly, and because of this they had the substance of things hoped for. Things unseen and eternal entered into them as the leaven in the three measures of meal, and in virtue of that they had the substance of things hoped for.

Noah saw the flood coming; and, in order to escape it he prepared an ark to the saving of his house. Shutting his eyes, and listening in his heart to the Lord, he might say, 'I hear thee speaking, most merciful one. Something has come into me, and I see in advance one hundred and twenty years. I see the clouds gathering, the flood coming and bursting on the earth. I see the ark and its measurements as thou dost direct. I desire to tremble at thy word, to submit anew to thee, to count all things but dross and dung for the excellency of thy glory, and to adore thy name for enabling me to obey the form of doctrine given to me.'

Being not a forgetful hearer, but a doer of the word, this man was blessed in his deed. He believed the Lord. That is grace reigning through righteousness, so that even outwardly he walked by faith. Though the sinful generation in which he lived were restrained from murdering him he would, no doubt, be the laughing stock and, like the Redeemer, the song of vile drunkards. Yet he could say:

> *And I will constantly go on*
> *in strength of God the Lord;*
> *And thine own righteousness, ev'n thine*
> *alone, I will record.*

Many, no doubt, would have helped in the building of the ark, and may have been well paid for it, but there was always this invisible wall between Noah and them. Noah believed the word of God, and they did not. He was a well of love, zeal and ardour, although unbelief might whisper in his ear, 'Perhaps these prophecies will never be fulfilled'. The Lord would come with more grace, and more grace. He saw the God of glory, and the glory of God. There was faith — moved with fear, he did what he did, and he is in glory now.

The woman of Samaria

The woman of Samaria is an example of one building on
the sand. When Christ spoke to her she would not listen
and her attitude was 'I'll have the last word'. She had her two
arms round the sand, and was wriggling into it. And Christ
bore with her, and bore with her, until the Father said, 'Send
that dove that I gave you into her heart.' Then she was
stunned and astounded. 'Thou art the Messiah; thou art the
Rose of Sharon, the altogether lovely one.'

Afterwards she would say, 'It's a wonder how he bore
with me — it's a wonder that he did not get a stick to hit
me with!' Then she left her water pot (I wonder if she
ever went back for it — perhaps we should not enquire
into these things); she ran and told others about him. They
came and heard him for themselves and said 'Now we believe;
you don't need to tell us; we know ourselves.' Then they
said to Christ 'Stay a while with us'. I am sure he would
have been put up very well; we read that he stayed there
two days.

*I will allure her and bring her into the wilderness and speak
comfortably to her.* (Hosea 2:14)
    The woman of Samaria is an example of one to whom
we might apply this truth — 'I will allure her'. Christ said
to her 'I will allure you'. He brought her into the wilderness. Perhaps there were men looking on, but she was
brought into a solitary place in her spiritual experience,
and so are all the godly.

She said to Christ, 'When Messias is come he will tell
us all things'. They claimed Jacob as their father. They
had what we may call a garbled version of the Pentateuch,
and they were looking for the day when the word would
be fulfilled '. . . until Shiloh come, and to him shall the
gathering of the people be.' She was saying in fact, 'I am
going to wash my hands of you'. You can just see her there
with her waterpot, tilting her head at him. But then he
said, 'I that speak unto thee am he'. And he gave her something which you do not hear perhaps often referred to —

and indeed it is a delicate subject to handle — the testimony
of the Holy Spirit. She did not know it, but he gave her,
with that word, 'I that speak unto thee am he', the in-
scrutable, irresistible, grace of the Holy Spirit. And that
would not leave her to all eternity, though at the time she
would not know all that was involved in being united to
Christ. Now this was of course a divine alluring, not common
grace.

He said to her, 'I will give you the valley of Achor for a
door of hope.' The valley of Achor was the main gateway
into the land of promise. So Christ became her door of
hope into the covenants of promise, and the promises of
the covenant.

The ten lepers who were cleansed

These men stood afar off. They would have lived in a hut,
or tent, outside the village, so that they would not come in
contact with other men.

Christ told them to go and show themselves to the priests.
Perhaps they began to go towards Jerusalem. Of course
there were many priests throughout Israel, not serving their
course at Jerusalem. If they asked, they would soon be told
where a priest was — or perhaps they themselves knew
where to find one. Anyway they were very obedient, and
went immediately to carry out Christ's command. We do
not read that they were questioning what Christ told them
to do, and doubting it; they went obediently on their way.

'And as they went they were healed.' Perhaps this was
only half a mile along the way; perhaps it was ten miles.
Perhaps, if they were going to Jerusalem, it was just as
they came near the temple — we are not told, and we do
not know. But at any rate, as they were walking together,
one of them perhaps began to say to another, 'I am feeling
rather strange; I am feeling well.' And the other might say
to him, 'Oh yes, your lips are not swollen and bulging the

way they were this morning. There is not that white patch on your forehead that there used to be, there is not that yellow hair in the scab, or in the raw flesh' (as we read in Leviticus). Perhaps they had an examination of one another on the road.

But one of them had to say, 'I am feeling better in my body, but I am feeling sick in my soul.' What do you mean? That is somewhat paradoxical. I mean that he was sick of love. You might say to this Samaritan, 'That man was your balm of Gilead'. He would say, 'Yes, he is my *Royal Infirmary*'.

This man was a Samaritan. Perhaps if he got the length of the priest the priest would only despise him for not being a Jew. He would likely not know much of the Bible. Likely he might only know odds and ends of verses. Yet although he might not know the words of Psalm 103 he would be able now to say, 'Who thy diseases all and pains doth heal, and thee relieve'. And he could say, 'I am sick of love in my soul for that man. I see his glory and I must go away back to worship him.'

The woman with the issue of blood

Very likely, when speaking of the woman who came with the issue of blood, we should keep in mind the distinction between saving faith and the faith of miracles. She came to know that this prophet of Nazareth had healed lepers, had raised the dead, and so on. The usual view is that when she came with the faith of miracles she had saving faith as well. But I have doubts about that. She was what you would call a long-headed woman. She was crafty, and the Lord had given her that. She had a plan made up that if she would get in between, say, a couple of disciples and reach her hand to touch the fringe of his robe she would be healed. And so it worked out, and then she tried to get away.

But the Redeemer was entirely acquaint with all her ways.

He sent his word after her and arrested her. He did not have to send two men, or four, or six to hold her; but she heard his word and that was enough. She was stopped. Now this was the turning point, when she passed into a new creature. She realised that this was the Lord of Glory, and she bowed to him, as one who had told her all things that ever she did. Now he said to her, 'Go in peace; thy faith hath saved thee.' That was when she passed on from healing of body to healing of soul. Now she was under the robe of the near kinsman and had the life which shall never end.

Jonah

They that observe lying vanities forsake their own mercy.
(Jonah 2:8)
Although Jonah had little bits of thorns and briars sticking out here and there he was a dear child of God, and the dealings of the Lord led things right about face; and not only was the Lord against Jonah but there was another against Jonah, and that was Jonah himself. And the moment Jonah turned against Jonah, the moment that Jonah began to take the side of the Lord against Jonah, then Jonah got liberty.

Now at this time God gave this command to Jonah: 'Arise, go to Nineveh, that great city, and cry against it; for their wickedness has come up before me.' But Jonah's position was, 'I do not want them to get a warning. Those heathen — they do not deserve to get a crumb from the Master's table. Oh! that Judah would turn to the Lord, but oh, those heathenish creatures! If these Ninevites were only out of the way, if only thy judgments would come upon them, then we would have liberty, and we would not be taken away to captivity at all.' He was a God-fearing man, but then here is an example of lying vanities; the flesh was allowed to get the upper hand. And how the flesh is left in the people of God! 'The flesh lusteth against the spirit, and the spirit against the flesh: and these are contrary the one to the other so that ye cannot do the things that ye would.' Jonah was allowed to take his wisdom, his will, and his plan, and to pit these against the will and counsel of the Most High. (I am sure that, after this, drops of sweat would come tumbling down his face when he would think of this. He would come and ask pardon for the sins that were pardoned already.)

What did Jonah do? He rose up to flee from the presence of the Lord. He seemed to get out of it in a very easy way. The worthy man of God got a fair wind for a while, and you would think that he would get to Tarsus without any trouble (although I never heard that he ever got his money back). Well, the Lord allowed him to go so far, but he had a hook in him. Jonah was a good salmon, and the Lord had his hook in him.

But now, the Lord said that his time had come. You have first of all the storm. The Lord has the wind in the hollow of his fists, and he has only to say to the wind *Blow,* and it will blow. We cannot understand how, but it is the doing of the Lord.

Then you have the sea-sickness of Jonah (whether there was physical sea-sickness in it or not) that he might be brought to this: 'I have trusted in lying vanities. Oh, I put my counsel and my plans over against your plans.' Where did the sea-sickness come in? It was in his conscience. He had just sea-sickness of conscience and of soul. Where you have sea-sickness, you vomit out. And this godly man had drunk in what his spiritual stomach could not carry; and he was to put it out bit by bit, until at last he had to vomit it all out; step by step he was led on until he was brought to this: 'They that observe lying vanities forsake their own mercy'.

But when he came to confess *that*, there was relief. The Holy Spirit was operative in the whale's belly. 'Lord, I will look to thy holy temple; and Lord, I confess this, that I observed lying vanities, and I forsook my own mercy.' And he gave him pardon and peace there.

Paul

Paul persecuted the church of God until the Lord met him on his way to Damascus. 'Saul, Saul, why persecutest thou me? Why are you kicking against the pricks, Saul? You will get a cut on your leg.'

Paul and R. M. McCheyne would agree very well —

> *I once was a stranger to grace and to God*
> *I knew not my danger and felt not my load*
> *Till free grace awoke me ... ...*

It is *free* grace from beginning to end to both Paul and McCheyne. Christ was both treasure and boast — a treasure which moth will never get near to destroy.

This same Jesus was now the treasure and boast of Paul. To him the Lord said, 'Depart, for I will send thee far hence to the Gentiles' (Acts 22:21). 'Awake oh, north wind, and come, thou south, blow upon my garden; not to destroy it, but that the spices thereof will reach to Rome and Corinth, Asia Minor and to Dingwall.'

Paul is an advertisement for the grace of Father, Son and Holy Ghost. He was before a thorn and briar (and well he came to know it). But he was turned into a beautiful myrtle tree, and he could say 'For to me to live is Christ, and to die is gain.'

Now, what was Paul's faith? Not everyone is of the same special use as Paul was, yet every believer's faith is in substance of the same nature as Paul's was. You may say, 'Wherein did Paul's great strength lie?' Well, 'the conies are a feeble folk, and they run into the rock.' They rest in the rock, and they find safety there. Paul was a feeble man, but he ran into the rock, Christ, and rested in Jesus, and he found safety there.

It was 'the exceeding greatness of his power' which quickened Paul when on his way to Damascus, persecuting the people of God and thinking he was doing God service. He was plucked as a brand from the burning. Paul was dealt with by a vision given to him. Others may have different experiences, but it is the same Spirit who convinces, converts and saves. He saw the Redeemer, and was changed in the inner man of his heart, and got a nest in the Redeemer.

Paul had previously been pleased with his own ceremonialism. He was circumcised the eighth day, of the seed of Abraham, of the tribe of Judah, an Hebrew of the Hebrews, touching the law blameless. He thought he had a big bank account against the tribunal of the Most High. But he was not circumcised in heart. (The circumcision of the flesh was meant to show forth the need for the heart to be circumcised spiritually by God the Holy Ghost, so that the soul might fear and love and be dedicated to the Lord, and become a living member of the mystical body of the promised Redeemer.) When Paul's heart was touched by the Holy Ghost, and when he heard the words, 'Saul, Saul, why persecutest thou me?' his heart was captivated in mercy. He got a frame of heart from the Lord to close in with the ministry of reconciliation. 'All things are of God, who hath reconciled us to himself by Jesus Christ, and hath given to us the ministry of reconciliation.' This was stamped upon his heart, and he was to know more and more about it as the days went on. He saw that his bank account had gone; he was bankrupt for eternity. Yet he was enabled to see that God in the Redeemer was reconciled, and he cried, 'What wilt thou have me to do?' In other words 'I surrender. Help me with the totality of my being to surrender to thee. What a miserable fool I have been.'

God says to all such, 'I put this reconciliation, which is already effected by Christ, down to your account. I promise poor sinners this reconciliation. Now, be good enough to come to the counter and stick out your paralysed hand and sign here. Do not run out by the door, but come, come to my beloved Son, and with the hand of your heart put your name to this message of reconciliation.' May your prayer be, 'Help me in the midst of my unworthiness. Help me to receive thy beloved Son, and come confessing my unworthiness. Help me to close in as a little child with Emmanuel on his own terms, and be reconciled to thee.' When this takes place, in the twinkling of an eye, by lying down on the Redeemer, laying the whole weight of our soul with all its sinfulness upon him, we receive forgiveness, and Christ is Jehovah our Righteousness.

Onesimus

Philemon's slave, Onesimus, was brought into prison while Paul was there for the gospel's sake. Onesimus may have been guilty of theft and perhaps of other crimes, we do not know; but in prison the Lord met with him, and he too, became *a brother beloved*. He might say to Paul, 'Read over to me the epistles you have written to the Romans and to the Colossians.' 'Yes,' Paul would say, 'I will read them over.' Then, even though they were still in prison, they could say 'For lo, the winter is past, the rain is over and gone; the flowers appear in the earth; the time of the singing of birds is come, and the voice of the turtle is heard in our land.'

The Syro-Phoenician woman

This woman had saving grace — faith of the operation of the Spirit of God. She saw the glory of God in the face or person of Christ. All the godly experience this, although they explain it in their own ways. The Holy Ghost contacts them all. He touches their hearts, and gives Christ to them.

This woman was humble. She accepted the description of a dog. Not a wild dog, but a dog under the table. She had been renewed in the inner man after the image of God. Christ had called her effectually. This was the work of God's Spirit, whereby, convincing her of her sin and misery, enlightening her mind in the knowledge of Christ, he did persuade (through and through) and enable her to embrace Jesus Christ. 'Thy people shall be willing in a day of thy power.' Thy people shall give thee a freewill offering — a warm freewill offering — in a day of thy power.

Christ tested her faith — he answered her never a word. Again he said, 'It is not meet to take the children's bread and to cast it to the dogs.' She said, 'Truth Lord — let the children first be filled. Let the cities of Jerusalem, and Chorazin, and Bethsaida take thee, if they have an appetite for thee. There is enough in thee for them all.'

Afterwards, meditating on this, pasturing so to speak in these fields, she would say, 'Well, how he held me and upheld me'. He gave her the faith — he knew what kind of faith it was. Christ saw all the while that she had faith swifter than eagles to fly to him, and stronger than lions to overcome difficulties.

The woman asked, 'Have mercy on me'. This evidently has two aspects — on me and on my daughter. He gave her a crumb when he said, 'For this saying go thy way; the devil is gone out of thy daughter.' But he gave her another crumb. What was that? The Master. Had she not got him already? Yes, but she got more of him. David was crying 'Open thou my eyes that I may behold wondrous things out of thy law'. Were his eyes not open already? Yes, but we need it and David needed it, and this woman needed it more and more — enlarging of soul. If your eyes are opened you will cry, 'Open thou mine eyes'.

She would have had love and care for her daughter, she would have been praying for her. I think it right that not only would the devil have gone out, but Christ would have come in; Christ said to her, 'Be it unto thee even as thou wilt'. So, while the daughter was in the house, whether a hundred yards away or a hundred miles away it does not matter.

In dwellings of the righteous
is heard the melody

> *Of joy and health; the Lord's right hand*
>   *doth ever valiantly.*

Nicodemus

Whatever understanding was given to Nicodemus when he was first drawn by the Father to come to Christ, it is perhaps not for us to say.

One thing is clear, when we consider his case from the point of view of John chapter 19 — where we have the record of Christ's divine self-sacrifice, when he dismissed his spirit, committing his rational spirit into the hands of the Father, having finished the work given him to do, from the point of view of his positive sufferings — by the time that Christ thus laid down his life, Nicodemus must have had a great deal of spiritual, enriching insight into the holy truths which the Saviour had brought before him. These truths were like the leaven in the three measures of meal; or, again, like the mustard seed. He was well rooted and grounded in these truths. He was a tree, planted in our God's holy place by his almighty grace, when he came with the hundred pounds of aloes. By this time it had been given to him to follow hard after Christ, and he had good understanding. He knew a good deal of what it was to be born of water and of the Spirit, to have the washing of regeneration, and renewing of the Holy Ghost, if we may borrow the language of Titus. This is God's miraculous dealing, whereby the soul is begotten again to a lively hope, in virtue of Christ's resurrection from the dead, the Spirit washing him from his guilt, and uniting him vitally to the Saviour.

I do not say that he knew a great deal of the priesthood of Christ, which the Redeemer perhaps was referring to in John 3:13. But the disciples did not know much themselves, though they were in the Redeemer. When the Holy Spirit came officially, then they got an abundant entrance into the way of salvation. But still, Nicodemus had the good of it. When he came with myrrh and aloes, he certainly was getting a view of the Redeemer's glory, and he was a living member of Christ's mystical body.

It was as if the Redeemer spoke to him in a still, small voice: 'Nicodemus, you came to me by night, and now you know savingly these things I spoke of. You now have a new disposition, a new relish, a new taste, and you have passed from death to life. Now, come forward. Supposing your father and your mother are alive, and you have lands and houses, then you will come and openly forsake all these things, and your own life also; not furtively, as you did when you once came by night.'

Now, after the evening sacrifice, when the covenant was sealed with Emmanuel's own blood, he heard a secret voice saying, 'This is the way, walk ye in it'. And Nicodemus came forward, though they would strike him down for doing it. He was aglow with grace. The fire did burn, and these words he did let pass, 'I have here one hundred pounds of ointment; I will give it, and Joseph and I will roll up the body in it.' And if you had said, 'That is a great amount to give,' he would have said, 'Be quiet: shut your mouth, and put a padlock on your mouth. He is lovely, he is holily lovely. He cared for me, and I am sorry I did not come sooner.'

Nicodemus was brought to have the truth hidden in his heart, and by the time of the death of Christ he got grace to come forward. In their labour of love, Joseph and Nicodemus were like the garden in the Song of Solomon, full of myrrh and aloes, and the wind was blowing in on the two of them, bringing forth a sweet savour of love, holiness, self-denial — spikenard and saffron, calamus, cinnamon with all the trees of frankincense; myrrh and aloes, with all the chief spices. They got a faith's view of the glory of the revelation that God the Father gave his eternal co-equal Son to meet the curse and to suffer what we cannot understand, so that anyone that believes on him is not condemned.

The Corinthian believers

The Corinthian believers were delivered from the cesspool of iniquity in which they had revelled. We cannot blame them, for 'who maketh thee to differ?' As face answers to face so, if our eyes were opened, we would see the cesspool inside ourselves. But those who were born again in Corinth were saved from darkness; and in the compassion of Father, Son and Holy Spirit, were saved from revelling in sin. The Lord came by the Holy Spirit, through the Apostle Paul, and gave them 'an open face.' 'But ye all, with open face, beholding as in a glass the glory of the Lord, are changed into the same image from glory to glory, even as by the Spirit of the Lord.' (2 Cor. 3:18) Their face before was not an open face but had a thick veil over it, and the blessed Spirit came along by the channel of the atonement of the Saviour, took the veil off their hearts, and opened their understandings to let them see themselves in the mirror of the law. And when the commandment came they said, 'Amen, I am a slave of sin.' And when he tore off the veil from their hearts he let in the light of the gospel. Then, with unveiled face, beholding in the mirror of the gospel the glory of the Lord, they were changed into the same image.

In this world, these Corinthian believers had the earnest of the Spirit which shows itself in love to the truth, asking the Holy Spirit to enable them to understand the truth and pasture in it, to save them from their stoniness of heart, and being suffocated with thoughts of vanity. They also had this, 'Knowing that he which raised up the Lord Jesus shall raise up us also by Jesus, and shall present us with you.' Paul and the Corinthian believers, like all the Lord's people, were going to the Father's house. Their souls would immediately pass into Glory while their bodies, being still united to Christ, would rest in their graves till the resurrection. When the Saviour comes at the Great Day he will say to them, as he did to the disciples at the lake side, 'Children, come and dine. Come along to the marriage supper of the Lamb;' and death shall be swallowed up in victory.

7.
Quotations arranged under headings

Our need of Christ

To our shame we have to confess that there was a day when we did not know what grace is. We might have been saying pretty things to deceive others; but we were message boys to *Satan and Company, Wholesale and Retail Merchants of the Kingdom of Outer Darkness* — indeed we were partners in the firm.

When Adam and Eve sinned (and included in that were their posterity) they were like one that would come down on a rock — they fell there on that rock and broke their legs so that they could not walk in the way of holiness; and their backs, so that they could no longer stand before God with acceptance. They were smashed on the rock; they broke their jaws, so that they could not swallow a promise of Christ unless a miracle was performed in their souls. And if men continue like that, without receiving mercy after falling on the rock, then the stone will come down on them and grind them to powder.

Say to the Lord, 'My name is transgressor from the womb. I have broken my back and my jaws.' Wherever you have people who are secretly taught, they are given a new taste, a new insight, and they have forgiveness for Christ's sake. The lord promises them 'I will never come down to crush you like a stone. I will never say to you, Depart from me, ye cursed.'

What is the name of the river that lies between the Ethiopia of the old nature and the land of grace and mercy in Father, Son and Holy Spirit? Well I will tell you — it is the river of unbelief and the carnal mind. Engineers are very clever at building bridges, but they cannot build a bridge that will cross this river. You cannot cross it, either, on boulders or stones. The ferry-boat of self-righteousness will not do it. How then are we to get across? Jesus Christ says, 'I am the ark of the covenant. Depend on me, and you will go over the river dry-shod.'

May God grant that we do not go lonely to eternity! How appallingly lonely that person is who goes to eternity without 'The knowledge of the Holy, which is understanding' — without that which those have who are plucked as brands from the burning; that kind of insight and relish and taste, whereby they are pleased to hang their soul's salvation upon the Redeemer absolutely; not on a rotten peg which will give way, but on a nail fastened in a sure place.

It is a fearful thing to think of an intelligent man or woman going to meet death; if there be no comfortable reason to conclude that such a person had repentance, and was broken and prostrate at the footstool of the Lamb, and so brought in mercy to smell the sweet savour of the sacrifice of Calvary; and is now going within the veil, but without the Friend that 'sticketh closer than any brother'. What will happen on the other side of the veil if you have not got that? You will never meet the people of God or be with them, and you will never be with the Redeemer; you will be in a state that is unspeakable for an endless, endless, eternity where there is no January, February or March; no days, weeks, months or years.

Christ told a parable about a man who was going to go to war with ten thousand against a man with twenty thousand. Would he not be better to send messengers and seek conditions of peace? Now the law is to come out against us. Are we to say, 'Oh, I have ten thousand good deeds and thoughts; I will send them out against the demands of the law?' Oh, no! What are we to do then? *Ah, Christ, Christ, I fly to thee.*

The law came out against this man, Field Marshall Law. And Christ said to the law, 'Field Marshall Law, are you satisfied with me?' And the law said, 'Oh, yes, yes, you are on your way to Jerusalem, and I know that you are going to satisfy my demands there.'

'And now can this poor sinner go free?'

'Oh, yes, yes. I am very well pleased with him for your sake.'

'There is therefore now no condemnation to them that are in Christ Jesus.'

Christ's work of salvation

Adam was on holy ground, as long as he was in the fold of the covenant of works. But he broke down the gate of the fold, and went outside it. So that all the mere sheep, born of his race, were lost sheep. They were straggling sheep, wandering on the hills of the lust of the flesh — for example, the Jews and Gentiles Paul refers to at the beginning of the Epistle to the Romans.

Now the Father, sitting in the office of Judge within the Trinity, appointed his Son to be Mediator. (Christ, along with the Holy Spirit, is essentially God along with the Father. But, only in the matter of the mediatorship, he was subject to the Father.) He was anointed to be the good shepherd, who gives his life for the sheep. The liability of their sins was placed on him. So then Christ is able to make the blind sheep see. He puts them over against the gate of the fold, and puts eyes in them, so that they see the door into the fold, and they say, 'I see that gate into the fold, and that is the gate for me. It is a door that was crucified, but it will do me very well'. Christ is the door, and the fank, and the shepherd of his sheep. So that they say, 'The shepherd is everything to me and I shall not want, and I will dwell in his house for ever.'

God gave the Moral Law to Adam, but he soon broke it in pieces.

God said to his beloved Son, 'Thou art to be the second Adam, the Lord from heaven. You will be the covenant head of the church. The law is in bits and fragments'.

Christ said to the covenant of works, 'How are you? I'm pleased to meet you. I promise to satisfy you, I promise to give up the ghost to fulfil you.' He promised to gather up the fragments of the two tables of Moses with the worth of his life, and to hide them inside himself as the two tables were hidden in the ark.

The Son said to the Father, 'What is the bill?' The Father replied, 'Silver and gold will not do. I command you to lay down your life for this people.'

This is the great sacrifice for a lost world, and it is on the ground of this sacrifice that all are set free who trust in him.

The merit of Christ's atoning sacrifice terminates in the justice of God, and in the conscience of the sinner. Seeing his person is divine, then the worth of his death offered to me in my conscience to purge me from my dead works is boundless and bottomless and divine.

Although you would be swimming in the Atlantic Ocean of your own corruptions, Christ is able to put a loop of the everlasting covenant around you and knot it tightly at your back. He will pull you on to the *S.S. SALVATION,* and you will be safe on the way to glory.

Supposing you could think of a voltage on a wire of say 100,000 volts, or supposing you could think of an indefinite voltage on that wire, and it was kept at white heat and could not be otherwise — if a cloudburst came on that wire, what would happen? Would it extinguish the white heat of the wire? If we may reverently use this illustration, the Redeemer is in his human nature the wire, and he had infinite power at his disposal — infinite resources and fervency. And although a cloudburst came upon him, nevertheless, instead of the cloudburst extinguishing the heat, and the intense whiteness of absolute holiness and zeal, it was only the heat in the wire that extinguished the cloudburst and sent it up in clouds of steam, and exhausted the wrath of God and the devils also.

He would be a fool among men who would play with a voltage of 200,000 — he would be done for. And although the devils tried to do what they did in that way, they were repelled — they fell back in dismay — it was hopeless. It was his infinite resources that exhausted this cloudburst which came upon him.

One question which may occur to you is — Did the Redeemer finish the curse on Calvary's cross? In a very real sense he did finish the curse and the redemption which he obtained when he cried, 'It is finished'. You might ask, then, 'Why did his body have to lie in the grave, if the curse was already finished?' One answer is, because it was the Father's will; it was part of the covenant with his Father, that he should go to the tomb. But it may be appropriate to remark that when his soul went to Glory, the virtue of all his finished work went to Glory with him (though not in the supreme way till he ascended body and soul, when as the great High Priest of his people he entered heaven in an official, final way, to sit down on the right hand of the Most High). When his soul went to Glory, the infinite virtue of his atoning sacrifice was in him and with him there. And when he went to the tomb as head of his body the church, there also he took with him the virtue of his atoning death, to make an end of the power of death. And all his people were representatively with him in the tomb. A multitude that no man can number were with him as their adorable head. Untold multitudes were wrapped up with him in the aloes, myrrh and cassia in the tomb. There was no sting there. He had taken the sting out of death for all who believe upon him, when he took the sting out of the curse on the cross. And as Samuel Rutherford said, 'No worm came up on the body of the Redeemer'. He conquered the tomb, and yet he laid down in it until the appointed time. He was there during the last Sabbath of the Old Testament dispensation, as if to take it with him to the grave; and he rose again, bringing with him the first New Testament Sabbath, on the morning of the resurrection.

Election and the free offer

The Father gave the Redeemer a flock, and who they are we are not to enquire into; but we are to enquire into the Shepherd.

You may be saying, 'O but how do I know that I am of the elect?' Leave that just now. Can you say that the word of God is sweet to your taste, that you love the word of God? Well the word of God is that from which his people feed; and if you love it, you love Christ; and if you love Christ, it is because he has loved you with an everlasting love, and elected you from all eternity.

Christ is the bank, and Christ is the safe, and the door of the safe is wide open. The Father is saying, 'Come and welcome to Christ; in Him are hid all the treasures of wisdom and knowledge.' They will not send detectives after you, saying you are stealing from the bank. The bank door is open. The safe is full and you are welcome to Him.

Are you saying, 'I am afraid he will be angry if I come, because of the evil that is within?' No, dear soul, but he will be angry if you do *not* come. 'Him that cometh to me I will in no wise cast out.'

The law and the gospel

In our land, and in the visible church in our day and generation, there is a spirit of religious rancour toward the truth that man must meet the law. This is where the need of the gospel comes in, the unspeakable need that the Lord in mercy would raise up men who would preach the gospel, and be used to bring the visible church to the feet of Emmanuel.

The law is not an arbitary thing. It is embedded in the essential perfections of the Most High. Its home is in the being of the Most High, and in his essential perfections. If one is not free, spiritually free in virtue of the body of Christ, receiving what the body of Christ means, and embracing it, there is no escape from facing the law. Dear fellow sinner, if people would lay that to heart in Britain, Europe and Asia, how they would pray for one another, and seek lovingly to help one another. They would put first and foremost, not getting to the moon, or having armies and weapons, but the blowing of the ram's horn of the law, and along with that, in the love and kindness of the Lord, the blowing of the Jubilee trumpet of the gospel; that the divine Redeemer is righteously able to save to the uttermost from going down to the pit, because he is the ransom.

I am the Lord thy God, which have brought thee out of the land of Egypt, out of the house of bondage. (Exodus 20:2)

In order to reach the commandments, we have to come in through the Preface; and it is only through the Preface that we can keep the Commandments. The Preface is equivalent to, '*I am the way, the truth and the life*; come in by this way of salvation.'

The Preface to the Ten Commandments was a revelation anew of the covenant ordered in all things and sure. If we look at it, we shall see Christ as promising himself beneath and at the back of and all round each commandment.

We cannot love the commandments, nor God's works

in providence nor in grace without loving the Redeemer. The only way of approach to glorifying God is by redemption. That is the nest, and if we are ever to have spiritual understanding we must be little birds in this nest, and Christ's call to us is 'Open thy mouth wide and I will fill it.' The command 'Thou shalt have no other gods before me' can only be obeyed in virtue of living upon him; as Paul says 'The life that I now live in the flesh I live by the faith of the Son of God who loved me and gave himself for me.' By a Christ-given spontaneity there is a desire in the soul to say 'O how love I thy law'.

Faith in Christ

The outstanding blessing is to get saving faith, which is miraculous in its own way — our souls being raised to newness of life so that we be divinely enabled to appropriate the Saviour as all our salvation and all our desire.

We need faith to receive Him — faith of the energising of God. Faith is God-given. It is a God-given indebtedness of soul to Christ — a heart indebtedness, by regenerating grace; and those in whom this is found are dead to the law by the divine self-sacrifice of the Lord of Glory. They are then complete in the Redeemer, forgiven and freed from the law, the law standing and looking on, and well pleased with them in Christ. They are perfect and complete in him as to their state, being united to the Redeemer by this faith of the energising of the Lord.

I may use the telephone simply as an illustration. God speaks to you through his telephone from the heavenly country. When you are standing speaking to somebody on the telephone you do not say, 'I must see you coming in at the back of the telephone.' The person would not believe you. But the King Eternal, Immortal, *Invisible* is speaking to you through the telephone of his word. The lust of the flesh, the lust of the eye, and the pride of life cause spiritual deafness, so that we cannot hear what God the Lord will speak. But he can divinely operate in the soul so as to give supernatural hearing. When Paul's ear was opened he said, 'Who art thou, Lord?' And he replied, 'I am Jesus, whom thou persecutest.' Paul realised that this was God, and not man, and when the Lord opens your ear, the first thing he says is, 'I am God, and this is my word,' and the soul sets to his seal that God is true.

They hear his voice and take to Him by the secret impartation of life that shall never end.

The soul never lies down on the will of God in the plan of salvation until it closes in with the Redeemer. You put your arms round him, and he puts his arms round you.

Faith is the condition of getting experimental knowledge. However weak you feel, go out to the Redeemer saying, 'Lord, draw me and I shall run after you.' You will not be cast out. In the very act of your casting yourself on the Redeemer, grace will come to carry you on to the Rock.

Coming to Christ is not mere historical faith, but when the Holy Spirit causes you to see your need of the Redeemer, and enables you to close in with him as all your salvation and all your desire, then historical knowledge passes over into saving faith, and thereby the soul becomes an habitation of God through the Holy Ghost. When he, the Holy Spirit, comes, he draws the image of Christ in the soul; and from then on you will never leave Christ, and Christ will never leave you. You may 'faint and fail, but God will fail you never;' not even in the article of death.

Justifying faith is the first wheel, and once that first wheel is put into the machine (God giving the main-spring of grace) it will put the other wheels a-going — love to God and his people and so on.

How may I know if I am a true believer?

There is a partition between the living and the dead. Show me a godly man, and another man. However nice that other man is, if he has not Christ there is a gulf between him and the godly man. The one is in the land of the living, the other among the dead. The man without Christ would hiss like a cobra, if that was possible, in the face of Jehovah.

By nature men are like a lot of serpents hissing at law and gospel. The Redeemer says, 'I must turn these serpents into doves. I must impart a new nature so that they will begin to be ashamed of their own evil ways.'

Such have Christ in them the hope of glory. If you have reason to believe before the Lord that you got grace to turn against yourself, to say with Ephraim, 'Turn thou me,' then he loved you with an everlasting love: and such are here today.

The light may be very small. I see a handle here for putting on the lights; it can be put down to make the light very, very low. So it is with the Holy Spirit's work; it may not be very clearly seen, but when death comes and the Lord puts the light up — then in an instant believers will shine in the full blaze of light, in love and every grace.

The Holy Spirit makes the word a light to you; and when he does so, he puts a light in you as well.

There is a kind of invisible ink to be got, and you have to put the paper to the fire, then the thing on the paper will come out.

It is the same here. If the truths of the Shorter Catechism are written with the invisible ink of grace in your spirit, however you may be misunderstood by the world, or sniffed at by them, saying you are thinking yourself better than they (although you were trying to hide your head between your knees on account of what is within) the invisible ink will come out.

Where the Redeemer is received in a saving way, as the all and in all of the soul for time and eternity, a suitable measure of conviction of sin is implied. When God the Holy Spirit operates secretly and a sinner closes in with Christ for pardon of his innumerable transgressions, then the Saviour becomes precious, as he was to Nathanael and to Peter. He becomes the righteousness of the soul. This means there must have been conviction beforehand. 'The whole need not the physician but they that are sick.'

Conviction and conversion are distinguishable, but not separable. If you are a debtor to Christ you must have had conviction, even though Satan may harass you with the suggestion that you have not been convinced of sin, because you have not experienced the same terrors from the law as some of the Lord's people have passed through. If you are a debtor to Christ, you must have had conviction.

What is important is not so much the amount of head knowledge we have, not that we have read half a dozen or two dozen books, but the kind of heart knowledge we have. Are we in heart united to the crucified Lamb, and learning of him here a little and there a little? Many a question we might not be able to answer, but the vital question is this, 'What think ye of Christ?' If he is precious to the soul, then that person is out of the broad way, and into the narrow way that leads to life everlasting. Is Christ precious? Then, He has shone into your heart and has come in and will stay in for ever. That is the Holy Spirit witnessing with your spirit that you are a child of God.

Owen says that humility in the substance of it is not so much being sensible of sin, but mainly consists in being dependent on Emmanuel and the blood of sprinkling. There can be conviction of sin even in hell. If not joined to the

Redeemer and renewed to bear the image of the first born among many brethren we cannot go to heaven, the habitation of the high and holy one before whom the angels veil their faces.

Have I humility through the miraculous touch of the Holy Spirit, causing me to be dependent on the blood of sprinkling? That person is reconciled to the Lord in his own way, receiving the reconciliation offered through the Redeemer.

Perhaps you say, 'I fear I am not a believer, but O, I would like to be'. If you have reason to believe your soul is getting a bottom on the solid masonry of the finished work of the Redeemer and your soul, with all its wants, is lying down sweetly and tenderly — totally, lowlily, lying down on nothing but the blood of Christ; if you desire to be indebted to the Redeemer, and learn a little of him; if you have all your hope and confidence set upon him — then we have reason to conclude that Christ is precious to you and that you are of the city which shall flourish as the grass of the earth.

If you are rejoicing in the mercy of God and in the atonement of Christ, it is because you are a son of God. The publican smote upon his breast, and cried, 'God be merciful to me a sinner;' and in the word he used (be merciful), atonement was implied. 'According to thy boundless, oceanic mercy in the atonement, be merciful to me.' And he went down to his house justified. And if you today have the language of the publican's prayer you go out that varnished door, and out the big gate with the Holy Ghost within you.

You may say, 'You do not know what evil I have done in what I said and did not say, what I did and did not do. My sins are like the sand of the sea shore.' For the present, I am not concerned with the multitude of your transgressions but with this, 'The blood of Jesus Christ, God's Son, cleanseth us from all sin.'

Where the blood of sprinkling has been made precious, there is a secret leaning on Christ, a kissing of Christ in the gospel, a God-given reciptivity.

Where you are enabled to be indebted to him, you are born again. Guthrie has it in *The Christian's Great Interest*, 'If with lowliness of heart thou art satisfied with the way of salvation, the work of regeneration is passed already.' It shows itself in your secret willingness to kiss the Redeemer. That is a mark of regenerating grace. Where that is, you delight to praise the Lord. The scope of your life is to serve him. You desire in your onward way to glorify his name.

If you have reason to believe that your conscience is swimming in the ocean of the merit of the atonement, then you have reason to believe that he loved you, and will go on loving you.

All the angels in glory cannot cleanse the conscience from the guilt of one sin. This needs the uncreated Angel of the Covenant, the Son of the Father's bosom, set up and sealed from everlasting; and he promised to come and seal the covenant with his sweet atoning death, filling the heaven of heavens for all eternity, and may he fill your own and my needy soul this day.

Do you get a sweet smell of the divine efficacy of the Redeemer's atoning death, the reconciliation effected by the Redeemer? If that is working in you, dear soul, then you are in the everlasting covenant.

I shall tell you a story I heard lately about a godly woman who began to fear that she was loving the people of God more than Christ, and was saying, 'I doubt if I have any love to Christ at all; it is just his people and it is mere feelings.' There is a danger of that, too — having only natural feelings. And this woman was so afraid that it was mere feelings she had that she went to Mr James Matheson near Dornoch, and opened her mind to him. He was led to deal with her like this.

'There is a certain thing in the godly; and if you were sure you saw that going away, and that they never had it, then you would cease to love them and to want to be with them. It is because you are seeing Christ in the godly — in the broken and contrite heart — that you love them; and you need not trouble that you are not loving the Saviour, for you love him in them.

Perhaps you are coming to the means of grace cold and going away colder — mourning your lack of love to him. But your sense of ingratitude is an indication of your love. Perhaps there is at the back of your sense of coldness a spring of grace —'He is the altogether lovely one, the chiefest among ten thousand.'

The highest act of obedience ever rendered to the Father, or that ever shall be to all eternity, was rendered on the cross of Calvary. If you desire to love Christ for the highest act of obedience ever rendered to the Father, and rejoice in it, you will never give a scream in the place of woe to all eternity. If you are staggered and astounded at the grace which caused him who was rich to become so poor; if in mind and heart, with all your uncleanness and undoneness, yet you have heart satisfaction at the death of the Lord of Glory; then, not only has the blood of Christ been shed and offered to you, but it has also been sprinkled on you. Christ is *upon* you as your justifying righteousness, and he is *in* you the hope of glory; though you may be afraid, and seeing yourself so black. The promises are made over to you, and sealed upon you.

The life of believers

Feelings of unworthiness

Blessed are the poor in spirit for theirs is the kingdom of God; and blessed are those who have the kingdom of God within them, for they are poor in spirit. (There is a sense in which even the redeemed in glory are poor in spirit, for they shall be eternally dependent on him who loved them and washed them from their sins in the worth of his atoning death.)

A minister used to tell a story about little Johnny; that he fell into a well one day and the others went off shouting, 'Johnny is drowned;' and Johnny's uncle came shouting 'Johnny! are you drowned?' and he shouted back, 'Yes I'm drowned, I'm really drowned.' 'Well,' the uncle said, 'It's good it is yourself that is saying it!'

And that is the way the Lord's people are. They are often saying that they are drowned.

Perhaps, on your way home from the church, you will be saying 'Make the blood real to me. Make Christ real to me. I am a lump of ignorance, on my way to hell, unless under the robe of thy beloved Son. Bless the word. Make it real, and fulfil thy promises to me.' Before you know where you are, he is working in you, and you are building yourself up — though muttering and stuttering — and he will see to it that you will be kept in the love of God, and get the mercy of the Lord unto eternal life.

The believer desires to be rid of self-will and idols, and hates the thoughts of vanity, even though they rise like midges in the heather. If we have spiritual understanding and are members of the blood-sprinkled mystical body of the Redeemer, then we are perfect in the Redeemer, though weak and struggling in ourselves.

Growth in grace

If we will get the tip of the tongue of our souls dipped into the ocean of the merit of Christ, there will be a well of living water springing up in our hearts to everlasting life that will sweep away all the slime and filth in our hearts.

The old nature is appalling. It is like a house with many rooms, full of Philistines. It has Mr Self-importance, and many other lodgers in it. How we need the armour of the sword of the Spirit and the word of God against the Philistines in our own hearts!

Ask like a little boy who would go to a shop without a penny that you will get a pannyworth of manna for nothing. Keep from shops that will have a sign 'No manna in this shop — but we have something just as good.' Do business in the shops of heaven, growing in grace. And get a bag of nails, a hammer and a strong arm to put the nails into the carnal mind.

Believers grow downward into the word and upward to Father, Son and Holy Spirit in longings of soul; and outward to all nations, desiring that they would fly as clouds to the Redeemer, carried by the wind of the Holy Ghost.

Chastisement

God will never cast his children into hell — though he may, so to speak, put a measure of hell into them. But chastisement, however severe, is outside the boundary of the curse. He is dealing with his children, those who are members of his family, justified freely by his free goodness and grace.

The guilt that falls off when the soul is washed will never come on the conscience again in the same way. For when the person who was before a legal subject of the Most High under the covenant of works is justified freely through union with the Redeemer, then that person is not dealt with again as a guilty subject, but is received into the family. And when they contract guilt (as we do) they are not dealt with as mere subjects but as children.

And he will chastise the children, and he will make the dead flies in the ointment of the apothecary in your soul to send forth a stinking savour (and perhaps you will get living flies there too; but he will make the flies stink sooner or later). That does not mean he will forsake them. He will not cast them off utterly, because the Redeemer suffered for them. And you and I, unworthy as we are (and we are bad enough) if we are under the warm wings of the Redeemer, then

> *For sure the Lord will not cast off*
> *those that his people be;*
> *Neither his own inheritance*
> *quite and forsake will he.*

You are becoming like the Redeemer, however little you may think so. You are in the family, and are being treated like one of the family, although you are not perfect here below, and that is one of your secret sorrows. The Lord may take you across his knee and thrash you, as a father does to a disobedient child. Yet at the same time he will not say, 'You are no longer my child.' No, but 'You are my child, and therefore I will correct you.'

Attitude towards others

And he called his ten servants, and delivered them ten pounds, and said to them, Occupy till I come. (Luke 19:13)

Dorcas is an example of one who traded with the wisdom of a serpent, seeking to gather in poor souls. Many a woman can make clothes; but she did it from love, putting in a word to children and sick people and so on.

Paul himself is another example. He was saved from going down to the pit. And afterwards he could say, 'thy truth hath gained ten pounds'.

And are you using the pound? Not in an overbearing spirit, but taking a lowly place; not standing up on a great high rock, and saying 'Come not near to me, for I am holier than thou.' Ask that you will have Christ, and his truth; and seek that by unspoken earnest prayers you may be able to influence others. Seek that you will not be like the man who gained nothing.

Love not the world. (1 John 2:15)

What does he mean by the world? It cannot mean our fellow creatures as creatures. He did not say, 'Have no fellowship with the Galatians, Ephesians, Greeks, and love none but the Jews only, and have your own little circle, and hate others bitterly, and pray that they do not get the gospel.' No: he desired that, as the Redeemer wept over Jerusalem, so they should weep over their fellow sinners, desiring that the ends of the earth would be for a habitation of his Spirit and the dwelling place of the Father, Son and Holy Ghost. If we loved the Father we would love our fellow creatures as men and would pray that they would be brought from the shadow of death into the large room of the gospel to know the compassionate love of the Father, the condescending love of his Son, and the communion and fellowship of the Holy Spirit.

If you or I get a little drop of the love of Christ, we will desire that the whole earth would be filled with his glory, and that Jews and Gentiles would fly as a cloud and as doves to their windows, taking shelter in the clefts of the Rock of Ages.

Eternal security

If the gospel is divine to you, then God the Holy Spirit has sealed you against the day of redemption. That is *his* work, not mine. It is solemn work, bringing heaven into your soul; and he will see to it that it is carried on, and not one will be missing at last. 'Of those whom thou hast given me I have lost none.'

If you get a bite of Christ, you get a whole Christ. You cannot get one promise without getting all.

If we got a kiss from the Son, and are resting in a nest of a promise in the clefts of the rock of ages, the justice of God backed with omnipotence will never touch us. There is no such thing as the justice of God grappling with you if you have fled to this refuge. If you got a gracious flash of insight to see the suitability of the Redeemer who became poor that you might be rich, then clap your hands for joy and mark that day.

You may say that you have a little house and garden which you call your property. That is very nice in the providence of God. Still, you will have to leave that property behind sooner or later. Of late, especially, I have been thinking of how we meet men on the road with whom we may exchange a passing greeting, or they may even go the length of giving us a wave of the hand; and then, in a short time, we hear that they have passed away and are no more in Dingwall. They are lying down, and will not rise until the heavens be no more.

But the covenant of grace, sealed with the blood of Emmanuel, is the property of each one in this house today who seeks to touch the hem of his garment. If, in your heart, conscience and will, you can go on oath as before the bar of God that you are satisfied with the Covenant of Grace, then the whole Covenant is yours. Ask yourself if Christ is in you as the hope of glory, for the pardon of your sins, and for life that shall never end. If so, then the whole covenant of grace is your very, very own for time and for eternity.

> *God merciful and righteous is,*
> *Yea, gracious is our Lord.* (Psalm 116:5)

God is mercifully righteous and righteously merciful because of Christ; and if you put that in the pocket of your soul and take it out and eat it, you can go in the strength of that meat forty days, and not be put to shame at the Great White Throne.

It will not do to have a mere mental knowledge. We must be turned upside down and inside out. May your conscience sing of the blood, and swim in the ocean with no further shore — the plenteous redemption which is ever found with him. If you have that you have the earnest of the promise, and he will say to you at last, 'Come, ye blessed of my Father. I like to see you; I like to be with you.'

There are some here who are crying and groaning that they cannot believe in and love God the Father, God the Son and God the Holy Ghost. Believers cannot believe as they would like to, they cannot love as they would like to. They are mourning with a blessed mourning, and they have tears in God's bottle. At the Great Day, speaking reverently, the Father will hold up his bottle with those tears. He will say to those who shed those tears, who mourned over and were sorry for sin, 'Come, come, my Son has a crown for you.'

In Jerusalem they went up to Feasts three times in the year, but in Glory they go up once and never more go out.

Miscellaneous

The finger of God touches the heart, and the heart melts, and on the heart are written two words — *Jesus Christ*.

It is part of the sixth commandment that we flee from the wrath to come. Perhaps it would not be out of place to mention that even the excellent Jonathan Edwards has it in his book that we have no saving faith in the Redeemer unless we have a disinterested love towards him; that is, that we love him for his own sake. He went too far in that, and he put Dr John Love that was in Glasgow wrong, and put him into the ditch for a while. The Lord is not asking us to believe in the Redeemer only for his own sake — at least as far as I can understand it. There is a danger of confusing selfishness and self preservation.

Jonathan Edwards says that you must be unselfish, and that if you are only taking the Redeemer to save you from your sin, then you are selfish. Well, we are selfish, and there is no getting away from it. But at the same time we must bear in mind the sixth commandment, which 'requires all lawful endeavours to preserve our own life, and the life of others.' God is putting before you the principle of self preservation. He is commanding you to flee to the only Redeemer, who is divine and suitable for you, and on that principle you should take his protection and pardon; and along with that because he is infinitely lovely and glorious, and more excellent than we can put into words. The Lord forgive us for our sins in the want of love, and for our lack of zeal for the glory of the Redeemer. But if we are learning little by little, then we will come on like little children to love him for his own sake, and to take pleasure in him.

Seek to be putting on Christ. When you go to the tailor, he takes a piece of cloth and scissors, and clips a bit from here and there, sticks a sleeve in on this side and that. But, dear soul, when we come to be clothed upon with Christ, it is we who have to be trimmed and shaped to fit this wonderful robe which is to be the clothing of his people to all eternity.

Ask to be smitten with the blessed epidemic from the blessed country; that you could not stay in the land of Moab, but must fly like a dove to the Redeemer, and the Father in him.

*They received him into the ship: and immediately the ship
was at the land wither they went.* (John 6:21)

I am not fond of false spiritualising; but this may be a
suitable illustration of the truth that, whatever way the
waves are, if the time comes to favour a poor sinner, Christ
walks on the waves and the storms in heart and conscience
and says: 'It is I, be not afraid' — and he will bring that
soul to the shore of the better country.

Ask yourself, 'Is the Lord of Glory my shepherd and my
door?' Do not leave it to others to pray for you. You may
be saying, 'Is it not enough that DK and JT engage in prayer
for us?' No. Pray yourself that Christ be your Divine Shepherd, your Prince of Peace, your divine head. May you and
I have this prayer, 'Lord, save me from the devil and from
ungodliness. Turn me upside down and correct me, and
bring me to Christ. Help me to jump out of my own wisdom
and to hide in Emmanuel and in the blood of sprinkling.
Make Christ sweet to my soul.' This is the one who can
cleanse you for eternity. If anyone is in the Redeemer,
having his mind enlightened in the knowledge of Christ,
he will direct you to the green pastures, and make them
greener and greener to you. If Christ is precious to you
(and may he be) you feel yourself unworthy, and you got
a peep of the glory of Emmanuel as the way of salvation.
The language of your soul is, 'This is my rest, here still
I'll stay, for I do like it well.'

*Lord, save us from being choked in the bog of self-righteous-
ness.*

*Pour on us this day the Spirit of Emmanuel; so that,
in spite of our unbelief, we may confide in the
Redeemer. The secret of the Lord — his way of salvation —
is with them that fear him; and he will show them his
covenant.*

*O, possess us, possess us, possess us. Wash us and wash us,
cleanse us. O, renew that promise to us today, 'I will take*

the hard and stony heart out of their flesh, and I will give them an heart of flesh.' Put feet within our hearts that would run after thee. O, run away with our hearts.